S0-AEK-542

THE AGE OF VOTER RAGE

First published in 2018
Second printing, 2018
by Eyewear Publishing Ltd
Suite 333, 19-21 Crawford Street
London, W1H 1PJ
United Kingdom

Graphic design by Edwin Smet
Cover image by iStock, Nanos license
Author photograph by Jake Wright
Printed in England by TJ International Ltd, Padstow, Cornwall

The editor has generally followed Canadian spelling
and punctuation at the author's request.

Set in Bembo 13 / 16,5 pt
ISBN 978-1-911335-66-5

WWW.EYEWEARPUBLISHING.COM

THE AGE OF VOTER RAGE

Nik Nanos

NIK NANOS

is a Canadian pollster, data scientist and business strategist. He is the Founding Chairman of Nanos Research and has among the most distinguished records for reliability in research in the polling industry. He is the pollster of record for the *Globe and Mail* and CTV News, and also designed and oversees the Bloomberg Nanos Canadian Confidence Index. Nik is a Global Fellow at the Woodrow Wilson International Center for Scholars in Washington DC, a research associate professor at the State University of New York in Buffalo and the Vice Chair of Carleton University in Ottawa, Canada.

TABLE OF CONTENTS

DEDICATION

The current state of democratic dialogue in many societies is, in a word, troubled. The anger of voters is complex, with different causes in different democracies. The globalization of trade has led to change and put jobs at risk, while automation is replacing jobs of the past. Many people are unemployed, underemployed or getting paid less than they used to. It should be no wonder that some feel as if the establishment has fundamentally failed to provide either economic stability or the hope of upward income mobility. The outcome of this lack of faith is a lashing out at politicians, governments, businesses and the like, and a searching out of anti-establishment candidates who whip up citizens and mobilize the angry vote to punish the establishment.

As a researcher and observer of public opinion, I am often inspired by the nuance and sophistication of the views of citizens. However, the emergence of fake news, the increasing fuzziness of the truth and the economic despair and anger of the marginalized are rewiring democracy and reshaping public opinion. The new battlegrounds are not in town halls and neighbourhoods, but on social media and the Internet, ready to be manipulated and disrupted by anyone so inclined.

Though unpopular with some, I dedicate this book to journalists. I believe the only thing standing between the truth and a lie in our democracies today is a journalist. The courts are too slow to correct politicians mid-stride in a campaign, and expecting politicians to self-correct is delusional – that leaves journalists as the seekers and frontline protectors of the truth. This is not an easy task. In a world where the business model for quality news is under threat, journalists and news organizations have to recapture the confidence of citizens and cut a clear line between news opinion and news fact.

I have no answers, but I do have a deep respect for journalism as a profession and a hope that journalists can be the impartial vanguard to help citizens make informed decisions. Wishful thinking? Perhaps.

INTRODUCTION

'Inconceivable!' That single word encapsulates the thoughts of many about the current state of democracy. Donald Trump is president of the United States. Justin Trudeau is prime minister of a majority government in Canada. The United Kingdom voted for Brexit. Theresa May nearly lost the election to a newly-radical Labour Party. Emmanuel Macron quit the French Socialist Party, created a new movement and six months later won the presidency and a majority in the National Assembly. Each one of those events was an unanticipated outcome that rocked the popular political wisdom. Many of these contests were like watching a car crash in slow motion – with voters being strangely attracted and repulsed at the same time. For both winners and losers, there was astonishment in what just happened.

With xenophobic populism gaining momentum in numerous democracies, many have heralded the arrival of a new right-wing political wave. The reality, however, is much more complex than a simple swing to the right. Here we will explore the 'age of voter rage': how the marginalized and the margins are rewiring democracy. Rage is an intense emotion, ready to surface at the slightest provocation. It manifests itself in the seemingly mild-mannered and calm person who snaps in anger when something goes wrong. Like in road rage, one moment everything is normal, then the traffic system doesn't work, the traffic lights are ill-timed, the other drivers are behaving badly and a driver is furious because they can't move forward. Voter rage is similar. A growing number of citizens across many countries believe they can't move forward. Their desire for better lives for themselves and their children is seemingly being thwarted by a system that isn't working and by others who aren't following the rules. This is the fundamental unspoken truth. In this world, xenophobia and racism are symptoms of a more endemic malaise founded in economic insecurity, pessimism and anger.

Countries enter election seasons and everything seems normal at first. There are political rallies, debates, platforms, media interviews – and then something snaps and an unpredicted outcome occurs. Voter rage in itself isn't new. In its more classical sense, it is a common part of democracy. It is about changing governments. People want change when governments govern poorly, are in power for too long or lose touch with the priorities of the citizenry. In this case, democracy isn't changing or being rewired; voters just want a new path. But when people are enraged, they are more willing to be led by emotion and to take risks.

Why is this 'age of voter rage', then, a new age – or an age at all? When one traditionally thinks of a historic 'age', periods such as the Enlightenment, the Renaissance or the Reformation come to mind. Historically, they refer to times when some sort of evolution replaces the previous model. The Iron Age knocked out the Bronze Age, the Industrial Age transformed an agrarian society into a more technologically-focused one, and so on. What is emerging now is not just a change movement of angry voters, similar to those of the past. The very structure of democracy itself is changing.

Democratic engagement and democracy are being rewired by social media, fake news, computational propaganda and automated bots working to shape the political preferences of voters and play on their emotions. In the past, revolutions were generally mass movements of citizens rising against the establishment. In this new age, where politics are increasingly polarized, very small voter swings are having a disproportionate impact on outcomes and the leaders those outcomes produce.

Think of it this way – Trump won the Electoral College vote on the narrowest of margins in three key battleground states: Wisconsin, Pennsylvania and Michigan. It is estimated that a swing in 1 in 3,333 voters, if they happened to be in those three states distributed perfectly, would have remade the outcome of the Electoral College from a Trump to a Hillary Clinton victory. That tiny margin was influenced by new forces. According to academic research from the Oxford Internet Institute, half the news people shared on social media in Michigan was fake, and the other half professional.[1] Fake news is

1 Howard, P.N, Kollanyi, B., Bolsover, G., Bradshaw, S. & Neudert, L. M. Junk News and Bots during the U.S. Election: What Were Michigan Voters Sharing Over Twitter? (2017).

not a fringe phenomenon; it is entering the mainstream, and a key source of information for an increasing number of citizens. Factor in razor-thin swings in opinion shaping democratic outcomes and we have a new age upon us. The twist is that those who feel economically marginalized can turn to the ideological political margins on both the right, the left or even the moderate center. It is about sending a message to the establishment. Coupled with the tyranny of small numbers, where small swings influence outcomes, and technology, democratic dialogue and democracy are being rewired. The mix between these forces are unique to each country – one common element, however, is the increasing importance of technology-enabled algorithms designed to disrupt and/or influence democratic outcomes.

In the pre-Internet age, elections generally centred around a common set of agreed-upon facts – whether related to jobs, the standard of living, the prevalence of racism or the level of crime in neighbourhoods. The facts were agreed to by opponents, fact-checked, curated and spread by the media. Politicians battled over competing visions to solve the problems facing a nation. Fast forward to the age of open information on the Internet and there is an increasing fuzziness between fact and fiction. One can make up facts, post them on the World Wide Web, and if they spread, presto – they are real. What is also real is how the Internet has helped mobilize and give a voice to those on the economic margins, or those who feel marginalized by the establishment. They feel the establishment has failed them. It should not be a surprise that around the world and in most countries, citizens trust institutions and professions much less than their parents did. Uncertainty breeds mistrust.

Citizens who are on the economic margins or who feel marginalized by the establishment are gripped by real world issues: Do I have a job? Am I underemployed? Can I keep pace with the rising cost of living? Their concerns go beyond not being able to enjoy the same standard of living as their parents, or not being able to afford a university or college education without going monstrously in debt. They are concerned with their ability to survive.

As a public-opinion researcher and a social scientist, I rely on data to reach my conclusions. I'll explore this research, much of which is in the public domain, from the viewpoint of a practitioner. This will help explain the true fragility of electoral outcomes, the proportionality of impact in these shifts and the effects of cutting through traditional divisions in society. Perhaps the most frightening take-away for some may be the suggestion that infinitesimal swings in the mood of voters could have changed, reversed or reshaped every single one of those 'inconceivable' outcomes. This new age of voter rage is driven by small swings of voters who feel marginalized, and it is fueled by technology. The approach in this book will be to cut across a series of elections and votes in the United States, the United Kingdom, Canada and France and to understand some of the commonalities in this new age. Admittedly, each chapter, politician and election could be books unto themselves. The purpose here is to scan political experiences across a number of nations and to present some ideas about what is happening and what should be on the radar for the future.

First, the chapter on Donald Trump and the US presidential race digs into the Trump winning franchise which included core Republicans, Clinton-haters and the angry. It explores how Trump used his experiences in the World Wrestling Entertainment (WWE) business world at rallies to tap into deep-seated rage in parts of the American population who felt that the establishment had failed – that Washington was broken, Wall Street greedy, the liberal media biased and globalization was a threat. Americans were still scarred by the Great Recession and the residential housing collapse. For those on the economic margins, Trump was the vehicle to punish the establishment. A look at the distribution of the popular support mapped to the Electoral College suggests that the very smallest of swings reversed a Clinton win in the popular vote to a Clinton loss in the Electoral College.

The second chapter explores the rise of Liberal Party of Canada Prime Minister Justin Trudeau. He charted his own personal path, separate and different from his father, former Prime Minister Pierre Trudeau. Trudeau remade what was an establishment image on paper (being the son of a former prime minister) into that of a rebel, non-conformist politician. He partook in a boxing match with a Conservative senator and knocked him out, tilted his Liberal Party further to the progressive left and led a positive 'sunny ways' campaign against a hardened conservative government that had been in power for almost ten years. Many wonder whether Canada is an exception to the phenomenon we're seeing in a number of democracies. A look at the broader situation suggests that Canada was exceptional in being ahead of the trend. Stephen Harper's previous Conservative government played the politics of division on issues ranging from crime to immigration and the border. The Conservatives saw enemies in what they considered the liberal media, the courts, the bureaucracy and big business in Canada. This is very similar to Trump's self-proclaimed enemies. In that sense, Canada may be a portent of things to come but it is not immune to the divisions and economic anxiety found in many democracies.

Thirdly, the UK's EU referendum is examined. Here one can see clear divisions in the electorate based on educational attainment, with Leave voters having a lower educational attainment than Remain voters. This vote should also be of note because of the reneged promise to repatriate £350 million a week for the National Health Service if the UK left the European Union. This promise was reneged on within days after the vote, even though it was plastered on the Leave campaign buses. The other key takeaway from the UK result was the outsider positioning and anti-establishment tone of one of the Leave leaders, Nigel Farage. Farage was a common man's politician, characteristically holding a cigarette in one hand and a pint of beer in the other. His background (not being a university graduate or a product of the elite public school system), notoriety and irreverence cemented an anti-establishment persona for him among voters. In the case of the UK referendum vote, a very small swing would have changed the outcome and the political fortunes of Conservative Prime Minister David Cameron.

If the referendum was one unforced error for the UK Conservatives, the 2017 UK general election was another. Conservative Prime Minister Theresa May, the successor to David Cameron, called a snap election in the hopes of winning a stronger majority mandate in the House of Commons, in order to strengthen her hand during the Brexit negotiations with the EU. Although Labour leader Jeremy Corbyn was dismissed as too radical and too unwieldy to be prime minister, Labour came within two percent, or one vote in 50, from garnering as much popular support as the incumbent Conservatives. In that election, young people and Remain voters rallied around Labour, and a number of older voters deserted the Conservatives because of the ill-conceived 'dementia tax', which proposed taxing the estates of people after they died in order for the state to recoup healthcare costs. A very quick backlash had Conservative Party leader and prime minister Theresa May doing a political U-turn. Likewise, the tragic Manchester terrorist attack put a spotlight on May's tenure as home secretary and her cuts to policing. These issues put her on her heels – all the while, Corbyn's more radical 'we demand' campaign (proper wages, respect for work, a fair standard of living), fed off another wave of voter frustration against the establishment. Corbyn was the radical left outsider who nearly toppled a sitting prime minister destined to win the election.

The presidential and National Assembly elections in France in 2017 saw the established party system smashed by maverick Emmanuel Macron and his En Marche! movement. Although a Rothschild banker at one point in his career, he positioned himself as a maverick in his personal and political life. Macron's wife is 24 years his senior. He likes to kickbox and he was a Socialist Party cabinet minister. Like Trudeau, he was dismissed by many as too young to lead his country. Where Corbyn in the UK veered his Labour Party hard to the left, Macron, the former Socialist Party member, created a new movement that was neither right nor left leaning. Within the short span of six months he launched the movement, won the presidency and did very well in the National Assembly elections. Even with this outcome, his graduation from the first to the second round of the presidential race was very fragile. If a mere one in 20 French voters had drifted away from Macron in the first round, the complexion of the second round could have been a show down between the far-right Marine Le Pen against the far-left Jean-Luc Mélenchon, or a showdown between the centre-right François Fillon and the far-right Le Pen. In France, the populist-style politics of Macron arose in response to fears of the extremes doing well or even winning.

Our journey would not be complete without

looking into the world of polling and reliably measuring opinion, given the limitations of public-opinion research and the folly of connecting aggregate popular support to electoral systems. The benefits and challenges of changing technology, the timing of polls, the overall projectability and interpretation of polls are also explored. The key takeaway is that not all polling is equal. Some polling methodologies have a better track record than others. The timing of the fieldwork is critical to their ability to capture election outcomes. The growing practice of modelling voter opinion to attempt a more accurate measurement is fraught with risks, as the recent UK and US elections illustrate.

The two closing chapters roll up the journey. First is a top ten list of what was learned from the scan of what happened in the US, Canada, the UK and France. Then, the journey ends with a chapter on trolls, bots and computational propaganda. Building on the findings of the previous chapters, the final chapter delves into how technology is rewiring democracy in this new age of voter rage and how narrow many of those votes actually are.

Outcomes that close do not tend to a healing of national sentiment. They put a spotlight on divisions and can trigger 'voters' remorse', where voters, when reconsidering their actions ask themselves 'Did we really want that?' and regret their choice.

In the 2017 UK election, some voters had a second chance to register their views (or voters' remorse for some) on the referendum and Theresa May's hard Brexit.

As people in Great Britain watched the US presidential race, many likely found it familiar. American voters were angry, the anti-establishment rhetoric was very strong and the race was quite close. As in the UK, the day after the election some Americans also likely thought, 'What just happened?' In the 2015 Canadian federal election there was not the same sort of anger, but an anxiety-driven electorate turned to Liberal leader Justin Trudeau, who ran an anti-establishment type of campaign against a tired government. In that situation, the surprise was the majority mandate using a more positive style of politics, contrary to the more common negative attack.

In France, Macron positioned himself as a maverick and the establishment French political parties were punished. As a thought experiment, take what Macron accomplished and apply it to the United States. Imagine if six months before the US presidential vote, Trump quit the Republican Party and created his own political movement, which won the presidency and then held power in Congress. It would be nothing short of shattering for the established parties. One should not diminish how Macron has remade the political landscape in France. What is interesting is that even with his big victory in the second round of the presidential election, he continues to look to heal the divisions in the French nation and vows to fight extremism.

Small swings have influenced outcomes in the past; the new dimension now relates to the growing appeal of more extreme political movements and outsider politicians, bathed in a technology-enabled world where fake news, algorithms and automated political internet bots rule.

One should not casually dismiss the near misses of anti-establishment rage in Holland and Germany. In the most recent Dutch election in 2017 the right wing Party for Freedom (PVV) picked up more seats in the legislature. This is the party that proposed banning the Quran and shuttering all mosques. German chancellor Angela Merkel is seen as a bulwark of stability in Germany, Europe and the world. Merkel openly welcomed Syrian refugees, unlike many of her European counterparts. Although her party won the 2017 national election in Germany, the right wing Alternative for Germany (AfD) saw significantly increased support, from less than five percent in the previous election to almost triple that.

Creeping anti-establishment rage is still on the move and making gains. It is here to stay until the fundamentals in democracies are recalibrated. The fundamentals being that more citizens need to feel that they have a chance for a better life and that governments are opportunity enablers. The current environment is one where many people believe that government policies, like trade liberalization, do more to put jobs at risk than to create jobs. Fake news and the increasing influence of computational propaganda propelled by the Internet and social media lead to disruption. There's nothing wrong with disruption, but for societies to function well, democratic dialogue should have a heavy dose of the truth so that citizens can make informed political choices.

Setting aside the data and the arguments which dig into this environment, the journey also includes some interesting anecdotes ranging from how pro wrestling can be a model for political communications and what a dwarf toss has to do with societal morals, through to the wisdom of a Montana park ranger.

The age of voter rage is not a homogenous phenomenon. Each country is different, but at the heart of all these experiences are a heavy dose of anti-establishment sentiment, divisions within those countries and a concern that future generations will have a lower standard of living, all fueled by technology and computational propaganda founded on fake news and hoping to influence voters. This is an evolution, a very fragile evolution, into a new age of politics which can both strengthen political extremism and the forces of counter-extremism. Who will prevail? That is the unknown.

CHAPTER 1
How Donald Trump Dropkicked Washington's Solar Plexus

Professional wrestling lore says the move known as the 'flying dropkick' was inspired by kangaroos in the 1930s. It involves the attacker jumping in the air and kicking the opponent with both feet, and its first use was attributed to Jumping Joe Savoldi. It was dramatic, over the top, devastating and a crowd pleaser to Americans who loved professional wrestling.

The Donald Trump campaign was like a flying dropkick to Washington DC's solar plexus[2]. For those Americans who were angry, the Trump campaign was a dramatic, over the top and devastating blow to the political, business and media elites who, angry Americans feel, are out of touch and failing them. The 2016 American presidential election was a showdown between Republican billionaire and media personality Donald Trump and the Democratic candidate, former US Secretary of State Hillary Clinton. The divisive presidential campaign was capped with an outcome where Trump won the Elector-

2 The solar plexus being the pit of the stomach where the nerves radiate.

al College with a majority of 306 out of a possible 538 votes and Clinton's national popular support outstripped Trump by almost three million votes – a victory and a loss for both, so to speak. One estimate by Nate Silver suggests that if one in 100 voters in key swing states had changed their vote, the election outcome would have been reversed.

A look at the presidential race suggests that Trump was a catalyst politician who harnessed and rode the anger of America. The US presidential election was the perfect storm for angry Americans to punish Washington. It was a combination of residual voter anger, the celebrity politician (Trump) stoking that anger, social media as an enabler of rage, and his opponent (Clinton) being the target and embodiment of the Washington establishment.

The leader catalyst: Taking Trump seriously but not literally[3], or, what Trump learned from professional wrestling

Wrestling metaphors are a natural fit for Donald Trump. Not many may know that on the World Wrestling Entertainment (WWE) website, he has a 'Super Star Profile' that lists him as the former owner of Monday Night Raw, a 2013 WWE Hall of Fame inductee, and the 45th President of the United States.[4] Not only is Trump a WWE Hall of Famer, but he also nominated one of the

3 Zito, S. (2016, September 23). Taking Trump Seriously, Not Literally. Retrieved July 5, 2017, from http://www.theatlantic.com/politics/archive/2016/09/trump-makes-his-case-in-pittsburgh/501335/.

4 WWE. (n.d.). Donald Trump. Retrieved July 5, 2017, from http://www.wwe.com/superstars/donald-trump.

founders of the WWE wrestling franchise, Linda McMahon, to his cabinet to lead the Small Business Administration. His staging of political rallies during the campaign and his ability to tap into voter discontent and anger had many similarities to the staging of professional wrestling events. Pro wrestling is a black and white world, with heroes and villains. Opponents taunt each other. Underdogs claim that the match and the officiating are rigged. Spectators are active participants in hurling abuse at enemies and shouting.

For those estimated 15 million Americans[5] who watch World Wrestling Entertainment (WWE), tuning into a Trump political rally was a familiar experience. Trump diminished his opponents by giving them nicknames. Democratic presidential nominee Hillary Clinton was 'Crooked Hillary'. Republican challenger Marco Rubio was known as 'Little Marco'. Republican Senator Ted Cruz was 'Lyin' Ted'. He belittled and trivialized his opponents to elevate himself and did so in the manner of a professional wrestler. His opponents were the villains, and among Trump supporters, he was the hero, the independent, self-made billionaire, unbeholden to lobbyists and the Washington elite. During the presidential campaign, he claimed that the election was rigged against him and that his enemies were not only the Democrats, but the Republican Party establishment, the media and Wall Street bankers. His messaging as a candidate also followed the wrestling formula. He made spectacular promises. He

5 Indeed Wrestling. (1970, January 1). Indeed Wrestling. Retrieved July 05, 2017, from http://indeedwrestling.blogspot.ca/2014/07/wwe-viewer-demographics.html.

said he'd build a wall between Mexico and the United States and get the Mexicans to pay for it. He said he'd tear up the North American Free Trade Agreement (NAFTA), negotiated by Hillary Clinton's husband, President Bill Clinton, calling it the worst trade deal ever. When he made these statements, the crowds at the Trump rally cheered while Democrat-minded voters argued that his promises were unrealistic. Trump supporters digested the exact same statements as Clinton supporters and the media, but very differently. As noted by Salena Zito, 'the press take him literally, but not seriously; his supporters take him seriously and not literally.'[6] This duality is akin to the professional wrestling experience. When spectators shout in approval or derision at wrestlers breaking chairs over the backs of their opponents, they are fully engaged in the experience but know that the act of violence they are watching is symbolic, not real. For Trump supporters who took him seriously and not literally, it was the symbolic promise to build a wall to stop illegal Mexican workers from entering the United States that was important. The literal promise to build a wall was likely not as important as the symbolism. For the media and his Democratic opponents, the Mexican wall promise was a literal policy to be challenged and debated as unworkable. Trump cut to the emotion of the issue of illegal Mexicans and their, as he asserted, criminality and emotionally connected with his supporters. The Democrats, conversely, wanted to present arguments and

6 Zito, S. (2016, September 23). Taking Trump Seriously, Not Literally. Retrieved July 5, 2017, from http://www.theatlantic.com/politics/archive/2016/09/trump-makes-his-case-in-pittsburgh/501335/.

facts to counter Trump but did not effectively contradict the symbolism of what Trump was saying. The Clinton campaign, for example, looked to evoke counter symbols, such as putting a spotlight on the American Muslim family whose son was killed defending America, but they simply did not have the same impact or visceral emotional connection as the Trump messaging.

A post-campaign remark by Trump at a rally in Michigan confirms the separation between taking his comments seriously and literally. According to CNN, at one point in the rally when chants of 'lock her up, lock her up' were chorused, Trump said, 'That plays great before the election – now we don't care, right?'[7] After having won the election for president, Trump opposed the prosecution of his rival, Hillary Clinton.[8] This suggests that Trump used and encouraged the 'lock her up' chant as a messaging device to voters to convey the seriousness of the Washington political rot and to connect Clinton to the Washington establishment. While the messaging and the political rallies were the spectacle of the Trump presidential campaign, Twitter was its real battlefield. Immersed in a siege mentality with the Democrats, Republican establishment and the media as hostile election players, Trump used social media heavily to get his message out, stoke the emotions of his supporters and extend the Trump rally experience online. By the end of the

7 Diaz, D. (2016, December 10). Trump on 'lock her up' chant: 'Now we don't care' Retrieved July 5, 2017, from http://www.cnn.com/2016/12/09/politics/donald-trump-hillary-clinton-lock-her-up-chant/index.html.
8 Wright, D., & Wolf, Z. B. (2016, November 22). Trump flips, now opposes prosecution for Clinton. Retrieved July 5, 2017, from http://www.cnn.com/2016/11/22/politics/conway-no-clinton-charges-donald-trump/.

campaign, he had about 28 million followers across different social media platforms[9] including 19 million followers on Twitter.[10] This is in contrast to Clinton's approximate 11 million Twitter followers[11] at the end of the election. His potential to directly reach voters and followers was much greater than Clinton's. Trump loaded his Twitter feed with provocative tweets day and night – which fed a sense of raw uncensored authenticity. The sensational tweets further fueled and fed his tribe of followers and had significant reach. For example, among his most popular tweets of the campaign, which garnered 167,000 retweets and 295,000 likes, was this in response to Hillary Clinton: 'How long did it take your staff of 823 people to think that up – and where are the 33,000 emails that you deleted.'[12] In fact, by spending less and being dismissive of the media which were largely critical of him, Trump circumvented the establishment and fought his campaign largely through political rallies and social media – using traditional media and advertising much less than Clinton. The reality is that he had no choice. According to Bloomberg News, the Trump campaign raised $646.8M while the Clinton campaign spent $1,191M.[13] If the pop-

9 McCormick, R. (2016, November 13). Donald Trump says Facebook and Twitter 'helped him win' Retrieved July 5, 2017, from http://www.theverge.com/2016/11/13/13619148/trump-facebook-twitter-helped-win.

10 Trump, D. J. (n.d.). Donald J. Trump (@realDonaldTrump). Retrieved July 5, 2017, from https://twitter.com/realDonaldTrump?ref_src=twsrc%5Egoogle%7Ctwcamp%5Eserp%7Ctwgr%5Eauthor.

11 Clinton, H. (n.d.). Hillary Clinton (@HillaryClinton). Retrieved July 5, 2017, from https://twitter.com/HillaryClinton?ref_src=twsrc%5Egoogle%7Ctwcamp%5Eserp%7Ctwgr%5Eauthor.

12 15 of Donald Trump's most popular Tweets. (n.d.). Retrieved July 5, 2017, from https://twitter.com/i/moments/795695925566050304.

13 Allison, B., Rojanasakul, M., Harris, B., & Sam, C. (2016, December 9). Tracking the 2016 Presidential Money Race. Retrieved July 5, 2017, from https://www.bloomberg.com/politics/graphics/2016-presidential-campaign-fundraising/.

ular wisdom that money buys elections were correct, he should have had no chance against the better financed Clinton campaign. Trump completely debunked the popular wisdom about the effects of money, organization and advertising on campaign outcomes. Trump's 19 million followers were only the sharp edge of his insurgency on social media. With the retweeting of his social media missives by his followers, he could have hundreds of millions of social media eyeballs a day. While spending less than the Clinton campaign on traditional media, he was able to hop, skip and jump over the TV networks and the newspapers. In an interview on CBS' *60 Minutes*, he told host Lesley Stahl, 'The fact that I have such power in terms of numbers on Facebook, Twitter, and Instagram etc… I think it helped me win all the races where they're [the Clinton campaign] spending much more money than I spent.'[14] The Trump strategy challenged the view

Figure 1
Clinton and Trump Campaign Spending in USD
(Source: Bloomberg Politics[1])

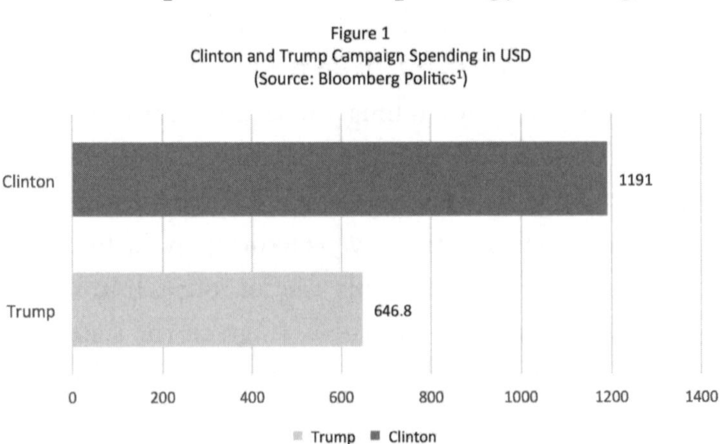

Source: Allison, B., Rojanasakul, M., Harris, B., & Sam, C. (2016, December 9). Tracking the 2016 Presidential Money Race. Retrieved July 5, 2017, from https://www.bloomberg.com/politics/graphics/2016-presidential-campaign-fundraising/.

14 Stahl, L. (2017, May 9). President-elect Trump speaks to a divided country. Retrieved July 5, 2017, from http://www.cbsnews.com/news/60-minutes-donald-trump-family-melania-ivanka-lesley-stahl/.

that candidates could spend their way to victory – effectively buy elections – on a number of fronts. Faced with less money to spend and fewer commercials and attack ads to run, social media was his preferred vehicle of choice to connect with voters. He didn't need as strong a ground organization to get out the vote because when one's supporters are angry, odds are they don't need the convenience of a ride to show up to punish the Washington establishment. In a sense, therefore, the Trump campaign proved that appealing to emotion and voter rage was a much cheaper campaign strategy than engaging and informing citizens of the value and rationality of a policy platform. While the media could fact-check the statements of politicians, social media was an open political market for both truth and mistruth. US Senator Hiram Johnson is believed to have coined the phrase, 'the first casualty when war comes is the truth' back in 1918.[15] Although many have focused on fact-checking Donald Trump, the reality is that both Trump and Clinton registered very low scores for telling the truth. According to Politifact's Truth-O-Meter scorecards, only 25 percent of Clinton's statements were true while four percent of Trump's statements were true.[16] Even factoring in the low score for Trump, the fact that only one in four Clinton statements were believed to be true is a sign of the state of political discourse. The Trump franchise emotionally

15 Who coined the phrase, 'The first casualty of War is Truth' ?. (n.d.). Retrieved July 5, 2017, from The Guardian, quotes https://www.theguardian.com/notesandqueries/query/0,5753,-21510,00.html.

16 Donald Trump's file. (n.d.). Retrieved July 5, 2017, from Politifact, http://www.politifact.com/personalities/donald-trump/.

connected with American voters and tapped into their discontent on a range of issues, including the loss of jobs to lower-paying economies through trade agreements, crime connected to illegal immigrants and the corruption of Washington. Trump had a platform, a symbolic narrative, an entertaining and seemingly authentic style and a segment of the electorate ready to accept his message. The conditions for a successful challenge to the Democrats were there and the election ready for the taking.

The anger: It can't be pleasant to come home to an eviction notice on the door.

By some standards, the fear of losing one's home in the United States is an epidemic. The Wall Street Journal reported that 9.3 million homes were foreclosed during the height of the housing crash.[17] A survey in September 2016 by the NHP Foundation found that three out of 10 Americans reported they were 'very concerned' that a friend or relative could lose a home along with another 27 percent describing themselves as concerned.[18] One should think of these statistics in terms of the human experience and the amplification effect. The irony is that years after the American real estate bust, the economy is performing much better – but the psychological impact

17 Kusisto, L. (2015, April 20). Many Who Lost Homes to Foreclosure in Last Decade Won't Return - NAR. Retrieved July 5, 2017, from http://www.wsj.com/articles/many-who-lost-homes-to-foreclosure-in-last-decade-wont-return-nar-1429548640.

18 NHP Foundation. (2016, September 7). SURVEY: 75% of Americans Concerned About Losing Housing. Retrieved July 5, 2017, from http://www.nhpfoundation.org/documents/PRWeb%20Survey%20090816.pdf.

of the residential real estate bust has lingered. Think of coming home and finding a foreclosure or eviction notice on your front door and the mix of emotions you might feel. At the same time consider how Washington endeavored to stabilize the markets and the financial system during the Great Recession by bolstering the banks. Nine million Americans lost their home while mistrusted bankers received bailouts and kept bonuses. In the United States, like many countries, their home is among the biggest investments that an average family can have. The loss of a home is not a personal event to be quickly forgotten, as the equity you thought you had at one point is diminished, if not completely wiped out.

Then, along comes a presidential candidate who tells Americans that the political system is rigged by Washington elites and the economy is rigged by Wall Street bankers. That candidate is Donald Trump. Now those nine million Americans and their families and close friends have someone who declares that it was somebody else's fault and that those responsible should pay for rigging the system. If one accepts that a home loss is something one carries forward, the amplification effect speaks to the reach of this issue. Assuming an average family is comprised of 2.5 individuals, the amplified direct effect of the foreclosure experience is 22.5 million Americans.

A national survey by the Pew Research Center titled 'Beyond Mistrust, How Americans View Their Government'[19] paints a very bleak picture. Between 1958

19 Fingerhut, H. (2015, November 22). Beyond Distrust: How Americans View Their Government. Retrieved July 5, 2017, from http://www.people-press.org/2015/11/23/beyond-distrust-how-americans-view-their-government/.

and 2015, the percentage of Americans who trusted the government most or all of the time dropped from 77 to 19 percent. One in three Americans who are or lean Republican and one in 10 who are or lean Democrat say they are 'angry' with the federal government. The angry Republicans and angry Democrats had Donald Trump to turn to. For the minority of Democrats, there was progressive Bernie Sanders, the main challenger to Hillary Clinton for the Democratic nomination. The key takeaway when one looks at the foreclosure and public opinion data is that coming into the 2016 presidential election cycle, the vast majority of Americans were distrustful of Washington, a significant proportion were outright angry at Washington and 9 million American families at one point grasped the dream of home ownership only to have it dashed through a foreclosure. Like the wrestling phenomenon, mild mannered people by day went to Trump rallies and vented their rage and frustration. They were told others were to blame and that Trump would fix things. Trump, spurned by the Republican establishment, opposed by the Democrats and derided by much of the mainstream media, activated his own new movement. Whether ironic or not, the Trump-nativist America First strategy was a call to arms.

The data suggests that the Americans driven by anger and discontent were there, waiting for a politician to come along. These Americans considered themselves economically and politically marginalized, so they opted for an outsider candidate, who had before never run for any elected office and who, one could argue, was even an outsider within his own party. It would take the miraculous alignment of the right politician pressing emotion-laden messages connecting to Americans teeming with discontent, as well as the smallest of swings in key states in the Electoral College to make Donald Trump president.

The numbers: How a swing the size of Bozeman, Montana would have made Trump a loser and Clinton a winner

On election night, it looked like the verdict was in – America elected Donald Trump in a close race, a significant proportion of Americans were angry and ready to punish the Washington establishment and the pollsters seemed wrong. In one sense, it made for very good TV. In another sense, what had truly transpired was not yet fully known. Not all the ballots had been counted. Beyond the win in the Electoral College, which in some close states took some time to settle, the rest was fuzzier.

Figure 2
2016 US Election Results
(Source: David Leip, Election Atlas 2016)

			Popular vote		Electoral College vote	
Presidential candidate	Vice presidential candidate	Political party	Votes	%	Votes	%
Donald J. Trump	Michael R. Pence	Republican	62,985,106	45.94%	304	56.50%
Hillary Clinton	Timothy Kaine	Democratic	65,853,625	48.03%	227	42.20%
Write-ins			1,129,478	0.82%	7	1.30%
Gary Johnson	William F. Weld	Libertarian	4,489,233	3.27%	0	-
Jill Stein	Ajamu Baraka	Green	1,457,222	1.06%	0	-
Evan McMullin	Mindy Finn	Independent	731,709	0.53%	0	-
Others			453,856	0.33%	0	-
Total			137,100,229		538	

As the results rolled in on election night, although the Electoral College looked like a win for Trump, the popular vote was much closer. That evening, American pollsters were on the defensive. The models predicted a greater likelihood of a Clinton victory in the Electoral College and had Clinton with about a three-point advantage over Trump in popular support. It was not until absentee and mail-in ballots were counted that the national popular vote polling was largely proven to be accurate. Pollsters estimated about a three-point margin advantage for Clinton in the popular vote and Clinton finished the race with about a two-point margin and almost three million more votes than Trump.

Considering the tone and focus of the Trump campaign, a number of observers pointed to race as the key division in the election. After all, Trump had identified 'illegal aliens', many of whom are Mexicans, in his call to action to build a border wall with Mexico. Likewise, during the course of his campaign he asserted through a tweet that African-Americans killed 81 percent of white homicide victims – an assertion which was fundamentally wrong and racially provocative.[20] This might suggest that the election was a race war. A look at the exit polling data comparing the two most recent US presidential elections suggests that race was likely a consistent vision in the American political landscape and that racial divisions in the Trump election were not exceptional. In fact, the Republicans enjoyed a 20-point advantage among

20 Greenberg, J. (2015, November 22). Trump's Pants on Fire tweet that blacks killed 81% of white homicide victims. Retrieved July 5, 2017, from Politifact, http://www.politifact.com/truth-o-meter/statements/2015/nov/23/donald-trump/trump-tweet-blacks-white-homicide-victims/.

white voters in the 2012 Obama/Romney showdown and the same 20-point advantage among white voters in the 2016 Trump/Clinton election according to the exit polling. Although the intensity of the race rhetoric might have been higher under Donald Trump, the impact on the outcome was no different than the 2012 presidential race. Race was an issue but one should not suggest that more whites voted for Trump in 2016 since that is not the case. Although race divisions in terms of voting intentions were stable between the two elections with a consistent gap, changes in divisions by education proved to be more striking. Among college graduates, the two-point advantage in 2012 for Obama increased to 10 points for Clinton. For those Americans who were not college graduates, the four-point Obama Democrat advantage in 2012 turned into a seven-point advantage for Republican Donald Trump in 2016. Educational attainment, not race, was clearly an indicator of the shifts in opinion in the 2016 election for president.

Figure 3
2012/2016 US Presidential Vote Swings by Race and Education
(Source: CNN politics, 2012, 2016)

Race	Election Year	Democrats	Republicans	Party Advantage
White	2012	39%	59%	Republicans: +20 points
	2016	37%	57%	Republicans: +20 points
African-American	2012	93%	6%	Democrats: +87 points
	2016	89%	8%	Democrats: +81 points

Education		Election Year	Democrats	Republicans	Party Advantage
Are you a college graduate?	Yes	2012	50%	48%	Democrats: + 2points
		2016	52%	42%	Democrats: +10 points
	No	2012	51%	47%	Democrats: +4 points
		2016	44%	51%	Republicans: + 7 points

Source: CNN. (November 23, 2017). Exit polls. Retrieved July 5, 2017, from http://www.cnn.com/election/results/exit-polls. The National Election Poll is conducted by Edison Research for the National Election Pool (ABC, CBS, CNN, FOX, NBC & the Associated Press).

The trends underneath the national result show the division in the electorate. According to the Pew Research Center, there were significant racial, general and education divides in the presidential election. Racial divisions were consistent with the previous presidential election but educational divisions were more pronounced. Whites, men, and those with lower educational attainment tended to vote for Trump. Non-whites, women and those with higher educational attainment were more likely to vote for Clinton. According to Pew, the exit polling pointed to the largest gap in preferences between college and non-college graduates since the 1980s.[21] Exit polling reported by the *New York Times* showed that Trump was competitive with Clinton among Americans making more than $50,000 annually, while Clinton enjoyed a greater than nine-point advantage on election day among Americans earning less than $50,000 a year.[22] The war was not between rich and poor; education was the important dividing line.

Figure 4

(Source: Edison Research, 2016 Presidential Exit Poll)

Education	Clinton	Trump	Other/No response
Highschool or less (18%)	46%	51%	3%
Some college (32%)	43%	51%	6%
College graduate (32%)	49%	44%	7%
postgraduate (18%)	58%	37%	5%

Source: CNN. (November 23, 2017). Exit polls. Retrieved July 5, 2017, from http://www.cnn.com/election/results/exit-polls. The National Election Poll is conducted by Edison Research for the National Election Pool (ABC, CBS, CNN, FOX, NBC & the Associated Press).

21 Tyson, A., & Maniam, S. (2016, November 9). Behind Trump's victory: Divisions by race, gender, education. Retrieved July 5, 2017, from http://www.pewresearch.org/fact-tank/2016/11/09/behind-trumps-victory-divisions-by-race-gender-education/.

22 Huang, J., Jacoby, S., Strickland, M., & Rebecca, K. (2016, November 8). Election 2016: Exit Polls. Retrieved July 5, 2017, from https://www.nytimes.com/interactive/2016/11/08/us/politics/election-exit-polls.html?_r=0.

The provocative Trump campaign style – focused on enemies (illegal aliens, the Chinese, free trade advocates, lobbyists, Wall Street bankers, the Clintons), residual psychological trauma from the American housing bust and the influence of small swings – created conditions for voter rage where the marginalized were mobilized. How many Americans were truly angry? The complexity of the vote decision makes that level of precision difficult to measure. One can conclude that the democratic dialogue was unusually angry and the outcome elected a president who voter rage and the swing of small margins made competitive with a better financed Clinton campaign.

A look at the historical trend line among presidential races suggest that most races are quite close (see Figure 4). This brings one back to the tyranny of small numbers. Every president in the past 20 years or so has been elected with less than a nine-point margin (which is a five-point or 1 in 20 swing). Most presidents are elected with an advantage of less than five percentage points. Getting one in 20 voters to change their minds changes

Figure 5
Percentage vote margin in presidential races
(Source: David Leip 2016)

Year	Democratic Party Candidate	Republican Party Candidate	Total Votes	Vote Margin (Number)	Vote Margin (%)
2016	65,853,625	62,985,106	137,100,229	2,868,519	2.09%
2012	65,918,407	60,934,407	129,237,642	4,984,100	3.86%
2008	69,499,428	59,950,323	131,473,705	9,549,105	7.26%
2004	59,027,115	62,039,572	122,303,590	3,012,457	2.47%
2000	51,009,810	50,462,412	105,425,985	547	0.51%
1996	47,400,125	39,198,755	96,275,640	8,201,370	8.51%
1992	44,909,806	39,104,550	104,426,611	5,805,256	5.56%
1988	41,809,476	48,886,597	91,594,686	7,077,121	7.72%

the outcome of every presidential election in the past 20 years. The key takeaway is that historically, these victories are much more fragile than the counting of the ballots and the declaration of a victor would suggest.

If that is not enough to show a small swing, one can consider the analysis of Nate Silver of FiveThirtyEight.com. In his post-election analysis, Silver estimated that if one of every 100 voters had changed their vote from Trump to Clinton, Clinton would have won the presidency.[23] In Nate Silver's world, this two-point swing (a single voter in 100 switches) would have tipped the Electoral College away from a 306-232 Trump victory to a 307-231 Clinton victory.[24] To put a finer point on the tyranny of small numbers, consider that Clinton lost Wisconsin, Michigan and Pennsylvania by a combined total of less than 80,000 votes[25]. These states make up 46 votes in the Electoral College. If Clinton had swung about 40,000 votes away from Trump, she would have won not only the popular vote but also the Electoral College.

In an election where 137 million ballots were cast, if 0.03 percent of the vote had changed (the equivalent from the total American population of about one in 3,333 voters who, if they happened to be placed in those critical three states, switched from Trump to Clinton), that

23 Silver, N. (2016, November 10). What A Difference 2 Percentage Points Makes. Retrieved July 6, 2017, from http://fivethirtyeight.com/features/what-a-difference-2-percentage-points-makes/.

24 Silver, N. (2016, November 10). What A Difference 2 Percentage Points Makes. Retrieved July 6, 2017, from http://fivethirtyeight.com/features/what-a-difference-2-percentage-points-makes/.

25 Zurcher, A. (2016, December 2). US election 2016: Could recounts change result? Retrieved July 6, 2017, from http://www.bbc.com/news/world-us-canada-38137630.

Figure 6
Clinton's and Trump's vote counts in Wisconsin, Pennsylvania and Michigan
(Source: The New York Times)

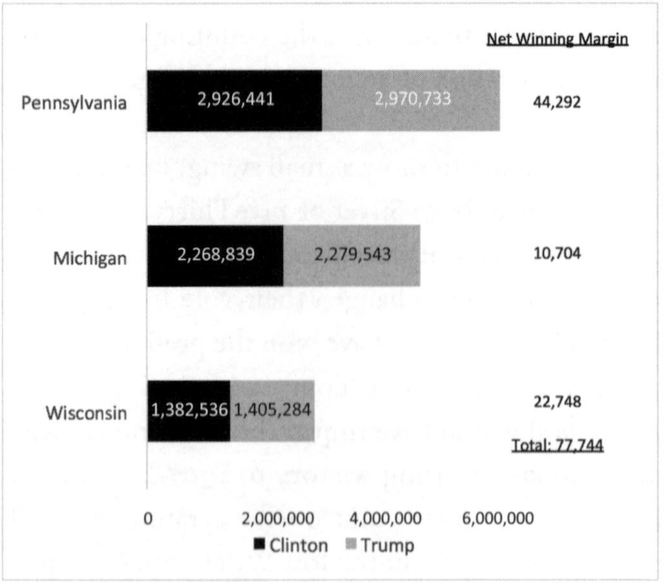

Source: 1 (August 1, 2017). Pennsylvania, Wisconsin, Michigan Results. Retrieved November 9th, 2017, from https://www.nytimes.com/elections/results/pennsylvania
https://www.nytimes.com/elections/results/wisconsin
https://www.nytimes.com/elections/results/michigan.

would have changed a Trump victory to a Clinton victory in the Electoral College. To put this into context, the population of Bozeman, Montana is 41,660[26]. This scenario is akin to the citizens of Bozeman deciding the outcome for the election of a country with 318.9 million people, of which about 137 million voted in the election. The recent election of Donald Trump is an extreme example of the tyranny of small numbers and how the equivalent of a rounding error change in political preferences can tip the balance in favour of one candidate over another in a US presidential race determined by the Elec-

26 The 2014 population in Bozeman, Montana was 41,660 according to www.population.us/mt/bozeman retrieved November 10, 2018.

toral College. Trump used anger politics to get into the game and be competitive with Clinton, but it was only the most fragile of voter advantages driven by voters who felt marginalized that made him president.

So, what should you do to win an election? Run against the establishment

A number of lessons can be learned from the US presidential race. First, the primary subtext for many voters was anger derived from a combination of forces – one could be angry over losing one's job to other low-paying economies, not be happy with illegal immigrants or Mexicans crossing the border, be angry over losing one's home or have the view that the political system was rigged by the Washington establishment, epitomized by Hillary Clinton. There was a figurative buffet of anger for potential voters to graze but what united the anger is that it was all directed at the establishment in Washington, on Wall Street, with the international trade order. Second, Trump tapped into and fed that anger with symbolic and sensational political messaging that showed that he understood how angry some Americans were. Third, because Trump had to fight an election against the Democrats, establishment Republicans and unfriendly media, he focused on rallies and social media to connect and mobilize his voters to be competitive with Hillary Clinton. Fourth, he stoked an anger driven by symbolic rather than literal truth. Finally and significantly, white voters without a college education resoundingly rejected Clinton. Education was a key dividing line, along with race and gender, that split Americans between those Trump attracted and those he repelled. In the final analysis, traditional political divisions such as race were consistent with the previous election – it was the swing of Americans based on their educational attainment that helped put Trump in the White House. Think of the Trump victory as a political cocktail – one part Republican core, one part Clinton-haters and one part driven by marginalized Americans whose political rage would turn to any candidate who was a vehicle to punish the establishment.

Donald Trump is a classic political insurgent. Never a public office holder, he motivated voters in an active revolt against the Washington establishment using Clinton as the symbol of the Washington elites and a broken system. At the same time, Trump was a political pragmatist. He said what he believed needed to be said to win the election and gave Americans an entertaining political show to engage and motivate them. Trump became president of the United States because a handful of Americans voted exactly in the right place and in the right manner to help him win the Electoral College. The last US presidential election was indeed the tyranny of small numbers.

CHAPTER 2
The Newest Canadian Path to Victory: Kill 'Em With Kindness

'Nice hair!' That was the popular Canadian Conservative retort to diminish the young, charismatic Liberal leader Justin Trudeau. Trudeau was an avowed progressive and loved to campaign. The naysayers dismissed him as being too young, too weak, lacking depth and coasting on the name of his father, Pierre Trudeau, one of the longest serving Liberal prime ministers in Canadian history.

His Conservative foes expected him to take the easy path. However, his journey to become prime minister would be very different from what the Conservatives expected, or even his father's own journey to 24 Sussex (the home of Canadian prime ministers). While it was informally marked with an event where he stepped into the boxing ring and knocked out a Conservative senator, his political strategy defied the popular wisdom of negative campaigning. He fought and won on his now proverbial 'sunny ways' positive message.

But first, to the fight. For those who have visited Ottawa, 'The Market', as it is affectionately known, is part of the city's original settlement. A stone's throw from the Canadian Parliament, since the founding of Canada it has been a commercial, social and political gathering place for the national capital with an active bar, food and pub scene. An Irish pub on William Street, Aulde Dubliner & Pour House, hosted the weigh-in for an unusual event. The Fight for the Cure hosted an annual charity boxing match to support the Ottawa Regional Cancer Foundation.

In 2012, the charity event had a political twist with national implications. Justin Trudeau, then a regular member of parliament for the Liberal Party of Canada, then the third party in the House of Commons, was to box Senator Patrick Brazeau, an Algonquin from the Kitigan Zibi Reserve, and a Conservative senator appointed by then-Prime Minister Stephen Harper. Brazeau, who sported a 'Brazznuckles Brazeau' t-shirt, was five feet ten inches, weighing 183 pounds, and Trudeau was six foot two inches, weighing 180 pounds at the time.[27] As the photos suggest, both were fit. Senator Brazeau's shorter stature but equivalent body mass meant his greater compactness showed more muscle definition than his Liberal opponent. Trudeau's acceptance of the match was contrary to traditional political wisdom and practice and anti-establishment in tone. Potential political leaders do not box opponents from other parties – even for charitable causes. Trudeau was portraying himself as a different, al-

27 Raphael, M. (2014, February 5). Justin Trudeau vs Patrick Brazeau: the weigh-in. Maclean's Magazine Retrieved July 6, 2017, from http://www.macleans.ca/general/justin-trudeau-vs-patrick-brazeau-the-weigh-in/ .

most anti-establishment politician – the strategy of risking a boxing match was more the stuff of an outsider, than the son of a former prime minister.

The media were transfixed on the spectacle of a member of parliament, a Trudeau and son of a prime minister, stepping into a boxing ring to fight. Many believed that Brazeau would mop the floor with Trudeau. Liberals openly speculated on the folly of the decision while the Conservatives eagerly awaited the expected political and physical knockout. For the Liberals, putting a potential party leader in a boxing ring with Brazeau was risky on both political and personal grounds. No political good could come of a Trudeau loss potentially validating the narrative of his weakness, not to mention the risk of being in physical harm's way.

Then, a funny thing happened. By the third round, it was Trudeau who was left standing. In the course of the bout, Trudeau let Brazeau throw his punches but then systematically wore him down, delivering a punch in the third round which staggered the Conservative senator. With two quick standing eight counts, the referee stopped the boxing match, and declared Trudeau the winner by a technical knockout.

This upset served to help reframe Trudeau on a number of fronts. First, there was the shift from being portrayed as a weak leader to being seen as more resolute. Second, it helped shape a more gritty personal identity for Trudeau, separate from his father, thus helping to disrupt the narrative of political entitlement the Conservatives were advancing. This progressive Liberal was literally a fighter and ready to put himself and his reputation on the line. He let his actions in the boxing ring speak. More importantly, there was the first glimmer of the Trudeau political strategy: to lower expectations and then work to exceed them. Faced with a deluge of musings about the risk to his physical well-being by entering the boxing ring – he did not respond to allay concerns – he let the lower expectations run their course, likely believing that he could either win or do respectably against the Conservative senator.

The key legacy of the bout was a new subtext that particularly influenced the media. Not one of the entitled son of a former Liberal prime minister but of the fighter-leader, an outsider, in this case, fighting the establishment Conservatives who had been the ruling party in Canada since 2006. For average Canadians, it seemed that there was something about this Trudeau that was different than they expected. He seemed like a political leader willing to take risks, scrappy, more resilient than some thought – a narrative more complex than the 'nice hair' quip of the Conservatives.

The sunny scrapper: From entitled scion to fighter for the middle class

If there is such a thing as a political scion in Canada, it is Justin Trudeau. One would expect his journey to victory as the son of a Liberal prime minister should have been one of the gilded political path – easy, effortless and storied. It was nothing of the kind. His rise to power was marked by a physical scrappiness, a positive progressive message and iron-clad message discipline.

The son of Pierre Trudeau and Margaret Trudeau, he had all the markings of a future career in politics. His father was a Quebecer, a long serving prime minister and head of the Liberal Party of Canada which had governed for much of the 20th century in Canada. His mother's family, the Sinclairs of Vancouver, British Columbia, loomed large on the West Coast political scene with his grandfather Jimmy Sinclair being first a member of Parliament in Vancouver and eventually in the 1950s a Liberal minister of fisheries in the federal government. Trudeau's father was a progressive intellectual and raconteur, global in his outlook, who did not suffer fools gladly. His sensitive mother, Margaret, is one of Canada's leading social advocates for mental health. He and his wife and partner Sophie Gregoire make a formidable political team – socially active on issues ranging from gender equality through to First Nations reconciliation, both media savvy, and together raising a young family. In a sense, Justin Trudeau is both his father's and his mother's son in terms of temperament and style. He seems to be both tough-minded and emotionally sensitive and has his wife as a political and personal soulmate.

The default narrative on Justin Trudeau, stoked by the Conservatives, was one of a party leader born into political entitlement, not connected to Canadians and not ready to lead Canada. The Conservative attack ads (using the 'nice hair' quip) asserting that Justin Trudeau was not up to the job had effectively done their work. Considering Trudeau won a majority mandate, the public opinion environment at the outset of the campaign in August 2015 should give one pause. Nanos tracking as to whom Canadians preferred as prime minister at the start of the campaign had Stephen Harper, the incumbent Conservative prime minister, the choice of 31 percent of Canadians; Tom Mulcair, the leader of the Opposition and head of the New Democratic Party, the preference of 28 percent of Canadians; and Trudeau, the leader of the Liberal party, the preference of 22 percent of Canadians.

On the first day of the campaign, Trudeau was the third choice, 9 percentage points behind the incumbent and six points behind the progressive left New Democratic Party leader.

One differentiator that the Trudeau Liberals sought to advance was a generally positive demeanor for the campaign – what is now known as 'sunny ways'. This guiding philosophy was first coined in 1895, by the

Figure 7
Preferred Prime Minister - Start and end of 2017 Canadian election
(Source: Nanos Research, 2015)

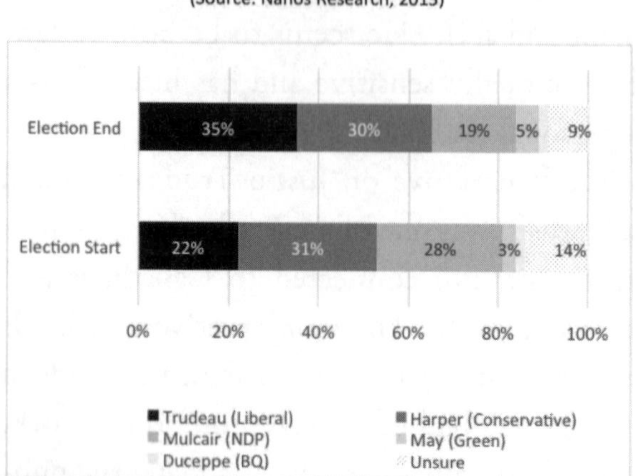

Source: Globe and Mail/CTV News/Nanos Nightly Election Tracking, 2015 Canadian General Election, national random telephone RDD survey, three day rolling average of 1,200 Canadians, accurate ± 2.8 percentage points, 19 times out of 20.

longest serving Liberal prime minister in Canada, Sir Wilfred Laurier. It is based on the belief that 'politics can be a positive and powerful force for change'[28]. While the Conservatives and the New Democrats ran traditional campaigns, focused on tearing down their opponents and fortifying their core voters, the Liberals ran an uncharacteristically positive campaign by Canadian standards. The tone was positive, the content was positive and the campaign tour experience was designed to be more aspirational. The Trudeau Liberal response to attacks was to remain focused on the positives. The Liberals threw a broad net, focusing on helping the middle class in general. Their platform advanced the idea that the top one percent of Canadian income earners should pay their fair share. Implicit in this Liberal dialogue was that the priority of Trudeau was the other 99 percent. In that sense, its objective was to ride a populist wave by trying to connect with the greatest number of voters both ready for change and concerned about the future and to decidedly tilt Liberal policy from centrist to centre-left. Trudeau's anti-establishment rhetoric took aim at a very narrow one-percent slice of Canadians. He would be the scrappy sunny politician, born to political entitlement yet targeting the richest Canadians for higher taxes with a very progressive message which squeezed the traditional left-wing New Democratic Party of Canada. Although many postmortems point to a progressive wave that engulfed the Canadian electorate, a look at the numbers suggests something

28 The 'Sunny Way'. (2016, January 8). Retrieved July 6, 2017, from https://www.liberal.ca/the-sunny-way/.

to the contrary. Yes, there was a progressive outcome and a majority win. An examination of the Canadian political context suggests that Canada shared common elements with the broader anger of voters in many democracies and it too was subject to the desire to punish the establishment and to small swings in voters having a disproportionate influence on the outcome.

Anxiety politics: The Canadian lighter shade of voter anger

Canada may not have had the seismic home loss of Americans, or the decline in true wages of the Britons or unemployment rate of the French, but underlying the environment was a fundamental anxiety driven by lack of hope. The economic narrative for much of the Conservative tenure in power had been much more upbeat. According to the Conservatives, Canada was an energy superpower with prosperity levers such as the Alberta oil sands project. The country had weathered the Great Recession of 2008 much better than most of its major trading partners. The homes of Canadians maintained or appreciated in value. Wages remained steady and the economy was generally stable. The Conservatives initiated stimulus spending through 'Canada's Economic Action Plan', investing in infrastructure, while keeping the finances of the government of Canada in a tight vice grip. The Tories framed themselves as deficit fighters. The story was that Canada was in good economic shape.

Figure 8
Bloomberg - Nanos Canadian Pocketbook and Expectations Indices
Source: Nanos Research, 2008 to 2017

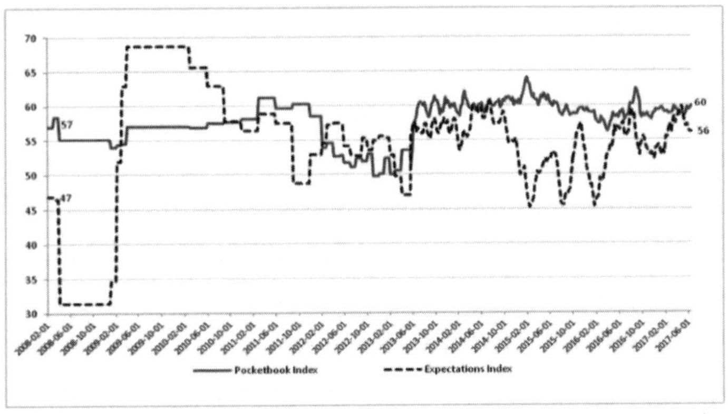

Source: Bloomberg Nanos Canadian Confidence Index, national random telephone RDD survey, four week rolling average of 1,000 Canadians, accurate ±3.1 percentage points, 19 times out of 20.

Even though Canadians might have been solaced by the misery of other countries as they grappled with recessionary forces, the perceptions of Canadians were less buoyant than relieved. The Bloomberg Nanos Canadian Confidence Index, which measures perceptions every week, suggests that at the onset of 2008, Canadians were quite worried about a potential recession – as noted in the drop on the forward-looking Expectations Sub-indices, which measures forward confidence. Eventually, the worry dissipated. Recession woes were for others to be concerned with, not Canadians.

Figure 9
Perceptions of Canadians on standard of living for next generation
(Source: Nanos Research, 2012/2016)

Question: Do you think the next generation of Canadians will have a standard of living that is higher, the same or lower than Canadians have today?

	2016 Liberal PM Justin Trudeau (n=1.000)	2012 Conservative PM Stephen Harper (n=1.000)	Change
Next generation will have a higher standard of living	14.1%	25.5%	-11.4
Next generation will have the same standard of living	27.5%	26.3%	+1.2
Next generation will have a lower standard of living	51.1%	37.3%	+13.8
Unsure	7.3%	11.0%	-3.7
Total	100.0%	100.0%	-

Source: Nanos Research, dual frame hybrid telephone online probability surveys 2012 and 2016, of 1,000 Canadians, accurate ±3.1 percentage points, 19 times out of 20.

More telling about the real mood was not how Canadians felt about the present, but how they felt about the future. Back in 2012, a Nanos national survey suggested that when asked whether the next generation of Canadians will have a standard of living that is higher, the same or lower than Canadians have today, only 26 percent of Canadians believed the standard of living would be higher while 37 percent believed it would be lower. In effect, only one in four Canadians felt positive about the future. The key takeaway is the disconnectedness between the hope of Canadians and the political narrative of the ruling government. What should give one pause is that after the election of the positive progressive Trudeau Liberals, the proportion of Canadians who were hopeful about the standard of living for future generations dropped from 26 to 14 percent. The lesson is that one should not confuse the positive 'sunny ways' of the Liberals with the views of Canadians or the mindset of voters. They were actu-

Figure 10
CTV-Globe-Nanos Canadian Federal Election Nightly Tracking
Source: Nanos Research, 2015

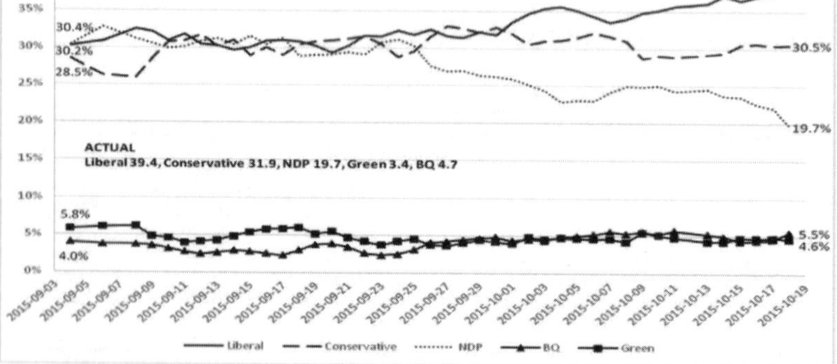

Source: Globe and Mail/CTV News/Nanos Nightly Election Tracking, 2015 Canadian General Election, national random telephone RDD survey, three day rolling average of 1,200 Canadians, accurate ±2.8 percentage points, 19 times out of 20.

ally more pessimistic in 2016 under the Trudeau Liberals than in 2012 under the Harper Conservatives.

Some argue that the last Canadian election was about values and choice and that voters embraced a progressive Liberal alternative to an incumbent Conservative federal government. The outcome was a Liberal majority government. A review of the data suggests that the election was about change with a feeling of declinism as the undertone – that future generations of Canadians would not be better off. One should exercise caution when projecting voter values and party values retrospectively on electoral outcomes. The election result was a combination of factors including voter fatigue with a tired Harper Conservative government, malaise about the future and what was generally recognized as a well-run Liberal election campaign with a leader, Justin Trudeau, who exceeded expectations. The Opposition New Democrats also attempted to run on an anti-establishment platform but that was largely rejected because they did not meet the expectations of voters during the campaign. One should be cautious in projecting a warm political embrace of all the promises of the Liberal election platform. This was a positive mandate for change and Canadians were ready for that change.

The numbers: How a shift of one voter in 20 propelled the Trudeau Liberals to victory

Among the more striking findings in the nightly election tracking by Nanos was the very high proportion of

Canadians who would have considered voting for either the NDP or the Liberals. A look at the ballot preferences trend line over the course of the election is not one where the Liberals gained at the expense of a number of parties but where the NDP and Liberal trend lines were mirror images of themselves. When support for the NDP dropped, support for the Liberals moved up. The 2015 federal election was about change and Canadians working through which party had the best chance to make that change happen. On day one of the campaign, Trudeau was the third preference for prime minister. One could argue that at the beginning of the campaign, Mulcair, the leader of the progressive New Democratic Party, was more preferable as prime minister than Trudeau who led the Liberals. The fact that both options were progressive in their party orientations made it likely easier for the switchers, unhappy with the Conservatives and worried about the future, to examine options and to then decide which party and leader had the best chance to unseat the Conservatives.

The economy was a critical backdrop for the Canadian political environment. The longer-term national economic data suggests a very strong relationship between the performance of the Canadian economy and the price of a barrel of oil. When the price of oil goes up, GDP rises and when the price of oil drops, so does GDP. This is especially true for major oil-producing provinces such as Alberta, Saskatchewan and Newfoundland and Labrador. As the election began, the price of oil had dropped, muting economic confidence. Canadians were not optimistic about the future and the Conservatives were a tired government looking to extend its mandate through a fourth national election victory. Factoring the high level of interchangeability of voter preferences between the two main opposition parties, the election was, in effect, a referendum on the Harper-led Conservative government of the day. The day to day solid performance of Justin Trudeau over the course of the election and his message, propelled by a positive style of leadership, made him the preferred agent of change against the Conservative establishment government. On the one hand, Canadians had the choice of a Conservative prime minister with a track record and a focus on economic and fiscal issues. On the other, a younger, progressive, Liberal alternative who had built his own brand outside of his father's shadow. This Trudeau brand was more populist, more positive and almost anti-establishment in tone through decisions like the one to fight a boxing match with a Conservative senator and the focus on the richest Canadians paying more taxes and openly advocating for government deficits. The boxing match allowed Trudeau to not only break with his personal past and a narrative of his own political entitlement, but added a dimension of strength and complexity that was not consistent with the simplistic messaging of the Conservatives. For average voters, perhaps Trudeau was more than the son of a former Liberal prime minister or a usual politician – he might be different, positive and welcoming but at the same time with the instinct and demeanor to win not just in the boxing ring but the political arena.

Although the parliamentary outcome was definitive, delivering a majority mandate in the House of Commons, one should not confuse the outcome of a comfortable Liberal majority government with a massive sea change. The data suggests that a small swing in opinion had a disproportionate impact on the outcome. According to the nightly election tracking by Nanos for CTV News and the *Globe and Mail*, during the last 10 days of the election, a swing of only one in 20 voters (five percent) from the New Democrats to the Liberals sealed the Liberal majority victory.

This provides context to understand the disproportionate influence of small swings in voters on election outcomes but also on the fragility of the election outcomes themselves. Going into the election, Canadians were not feeling optimistic about the future. It was a change election and the agents of change, in this case the Trudeau Liberals, were positive in their campaigning, progressive in their politics with an anti-establishment style of doing things. This should not lead anyone to conclude that Canadians are now more positive or progressive. The research post-election suggests they are now more pessimistic about the future under the Liberals than before. The conditions that unseated the Conservatives, namely anxiety about the future and the influence of small swings in voters, remain. When the Liberals seek another mandate, they could fall victim to the same anxiety and referendum-type anti-establishment forces that they rode to power.

History also presents a cautionary tale for the Justin Trudeau Liberal government. In 1968, Pierre Trudeau won the federal election handily, garnering 45 percent support over the second-place Progressive Conservatives who garnered 31 percent support nationally. This was known as the Trudeaumania election, in which Pierre Trudeau swept the nation and won a comfortable majority. Fast forward to 1972, and facing the same Progressive Conservative opponent, Robert Stanfield, the margin of victory for the Liberals dropped from 13 to three points and from a majority to a minority government. In the course of four short years the Canadian economy had slumped and the political mood had shifted away from Trudeaumania. A six-point swing, or the change of about one in 17 voters, rocked the Liberals, led by Justin Trudeau's father Pierre Trudeau, from a majority to a minority.

So the sunny anti-establishment can also win?

In contrast to the inexorable rise of Trump, some heralded the majority Trudeau victory in the 2015 Canadian election as counter to the angry populist trend. Justin Trudeau was decidedly progressive in his personal views, warmly embraced retail politics and was very media savvy. He ran a campaign positive in tone and repeatedly drove the message that his leadership was one of 'sunny ways'. The campaign was considered exceptional in one very clear respect – in an age of negative politics and virulent attack ads, the Trudeau Liberal campaign strategy sought to elevate itself above the negative fray. Trudeau presented a positive friendly alternative to a Conservative incumbent prime minister, Stephen Harper, who led a tired hard-edged government nearing 10 years of rule in Canada.

What is also interesting is that the Harper-led Conservatives whom the Liberals defeated ran a style of politics that shared some characteristics with the Trump phenomenon in the United States. Trump's self-professed enemies included the liberal media, the courts, and the Washington bureaucrats who controlled the capital. Canadian Conservative Prime Minister Harper had a similar list. In 2013, a leaked document purported to be guidance from the Canadian Prime Minister's Office to new cabinet ministers, bearing the title 'Our Enemies: The Complete List (Revised)' which included among the top three enemies of the sitting Conservative government the bureaucracy, the courts and the media.

The Harper Conservatives also stirred debate on the Muslim niqab, asserting it was offensive for someone to wear it while taking the oath of Canadian citizenship and had a heavy emphasis on the Canadian border and the screening of refugees and immigrants as potential security threats to the nation. This style of polarizing hot button politics was part of the Conservative political strategy for the past decade and had already been a polarizing political force used by the Canadian Conservatives.

Instead of thinking of Canada as exceptional, one would be better off to think of it as ahead of the trend. Canadians had already been fatigued by a Conservative government focused on division and driven by the belief that the establishment (the courts, the media, the civil service) were against them. Even with a majority mandate after two successive minority governments, this Conservative sense of embattlement against the establishment continued.

The Trudeau victory might seem counter to the idea of anger politics, but a look at the economic and public opinion data suggests that whereas Trump played hard and negative to activate voter anger, Trudeau mobilized concern about the economy and the uncertainty about the future in Canada behind an easy going and more positive-toned voter movement. This more positive tone was a response to a Conservative governing party which had a siege mentality, seeing enemies and security threats. Perhaps Canada is not exceptional but just ahead of the populist trend, where a previous Conservative and populist style government was rejected and replaced with a more positive Liberal party led by Justin Trudeau.

The lesson in the Canadian case study is that voter rage that comes from discontent or anxiety is not limited to the right and negativity, but also can be taken advantage of by progressives and by those who want to practice a more positive style of politics, unifying voters opposed to divisive politics. This is the sunny way of anger politics – a very Canadian yet lighter shade of the angry voter.

The other key lesson is that the Liberal victory was more fragile than the outcome in seats suggest. A mere swing of one in 20 voters in the last ten days of the campaign changed the shape of the election outcome into one of a Liberal majority victory.

I
EU
baby...

CHAPTER 3
What UK Independence Leader Nigel Farage Has in Common with a Montana Park Ranger: You Have to Burn the Forest to Save It

Let it burn! That was the advice the friendly park ranger in Montana's picturesque Glacier National Park gave as he walked along the burnt shore of glacier-fed Lake McDonald. The fire had ravaged the area and as the ranger hiked the trail, he explained that there are different views on what to do when fire strikes. One opinion is to fight the fire; the other is to let nature run its course. Those who want to fight see the fire as a threat to the flora and fauna of the ecosystem. Those who are ready to let it burn see the destruction in the wake of a fire as part of the natural cycle of the forest: it must be destroyed to be reborn.

In that sense, one could argue that the UK's convivial and controversial Nigel Farage is a disciple of the 'let it burn' political philosophy – that Great Britain's relationship with the European Union needed to be destroyed for it to be naturally reconstructed and rebalanced. The pro-Brexit forces would stoke Eurosceptic sentiment, be fast and loose with selected information, and let the firestorm known as the Brexit referendum run its course. One of the signature events of the referendum was a debate about the repatriation from the European Union of £350 million a week back into the National Health Services' coffers. Splashed on the side of Leave campaign's touring buses, it was a key flash point that galvanized voters who wanted to leave the European Union. In a world where political battles are fought not just on the hustings but by the Twitter hashtag, it was the uncorrected spark, questioned during the vote and later reneged, that lit a political wildfire.

The difference between forest fires and political fires is that many forest fires are naturally occurring, while these political fires were set, directed, nurtured and fed, culminating in a Brexit victory that few, even the Brexiteers, saw coming. After all, incumbent Conservative prime minister David Cameron had just transitioned from leading a coalition government with the Liberal Democrats to winning a majority Conservative government in the May 2015 British general election. The wind was in the prime minister's sails. He was finally able to deliver on his platform commitment to renegotiate Britain's European Union membership. It was about seeking a better deal for Britain. What was once seen as a deft political move to appease the grumpy Eurosceptic subset of members of Parliament within his caucus turned into a political mess. It not only put Britain's members in the EU at risk but uncharacteristically – and some could argue prematurely – ended the premiership of a prime minister holding a majority of the seats in the House of Commons and fresh off of winning a renewed national mandate. All this at the hands of an outsider politician, Nigel Farage, then leader of the UK Independence Party. Very comfortable with a pint in one hand and a smoke in the other, the once roundly derided and dismissed Farage went from fringe provocateur to unofficial victor on referendum night. Both his political opponents and the mainstream media in Great Britain watched on in disbelief.

Nigel Farage, Britain's convivial political Luddite

The Luddites were an English workers' movement in the 1800s who destroyed machinery in protest of changing working conditions in the textile industry. The workplace action and destruction was about getting better leverage with employers. The Luddite movement was more an attempt to rebalance the relationship between textile workers and employers in a time of significant industrial disruption than about anti-machinery ideology. The man believed to be the namesake of the movement – Ned Ludd – supposedly smashed, as a young man, a knitting machine in a textile factory in a 'fit of passion'. The movement, nurtured in Nottingham (coincidently the home of the famed Robin 'Steal from the Rich and Give to the

Poor' Hood) resulted in an outright workers' rebellion, violently suppressed by both employers and the government of the day. Similarly, the unlikely Farage sought to unsettle Britain's pro-Euro political establishment in order to rebalance the relationship between Britain and Europe. Neither the product of England's elite public schools such as Eton, nor of Oxford or Cambridge, Farage was not part of the 'old boy network' which dominates Britain's political establishment. He was anti-establishment. He went directly from Dulwich College, a boarding school for boys aged seven to 18, skipping university to work as a trader in the Metals Exchange in the City of London. Originally a supporter and member of the Conservative party, he broke ranks in 1992 because of Conservative Prime Minister John Major's support and signing of the Maastricht Treaty which led to the creation of the Euro currency and the further integration of Great Britain into the European Union. A year later he was a founding member of the UK Independence Party, went on to first be elected to the European Parliament under the UKIP banner in 1999 and to win the leadership of UKIP twice (in 2006 and 2010). Farage was the face of UKIP, a party once described by David Cameron as 'fruitcakes, loonies and closet racists'. Farage cultivated an image as an establishment outsider and survivor. His successful fight with testicular cancer as a young man was part of his personal narrative. Even his book, The Purple Revolution: The Year That Changed Everything, detailing his "cancer, a lemon-sized testicle and how the NHS failed me" suggests how irreverent his manner can be. In 2010 on Election Day in the UK, Farage survived a life-threatening small-plane crash after the UKIP banner affixed to drag behind the plane was caught in the tail. His personal political brand was one of being a survivor – someone who decided not to go to university, was not entitled, more celebrity than political statesman. His sights were firmly set on trying to disentangle Great Britain from the European Union. His fight was not only with the pro-EU Cameron-led Conservatives. In his own words, 'It is a war between UKIP and the entire political establishment.'

Farage's personal brand, notoriety and political message were well aligned for at least one part of the electorate: English voters who lived outside of London who felt economically left behind. Now the restless were asked to render an opinion as to whether to remain or leave the European Union. The benefits of the European Union, espoused by the political establishment and most of the mainstream media, rang hollow for some.

The rage: Take a 10 percent pay cut and please have a stiff upper lip

The British have survived much turmoil ranging from the spectre of the Spanish Armada in the English Channel through to the legendary 'Blitz' bombing of London by the Germans. Part of the national self-image includes a certain stoic attitude in the face of adversity. Great Britain had politically transitioned from having a large empire spanning the globe, being victorious in two world wars, through the Cold War between the Soviet Union and the United States when it was no longer a global superpower, to being the light-handed leader of the Commonwealth of Nations. Through that period of geopolitical change, one relative constant was the role of the City of London as a key financial hub in the world's economy. In 2016, the UK was the fifth largest economy by GDP according to the World Bank, with London holding the global top position in the Global Financial Centres Index.

Figure 11
Value of real estate values in London vs rest of England
(Source: Land Registry UK Government, 2007-2014)

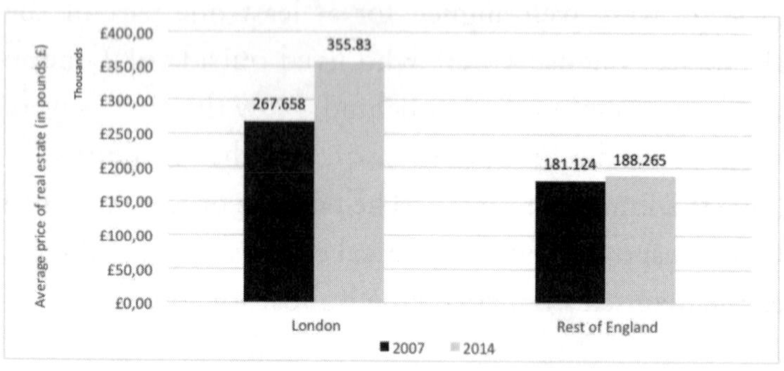

Source: House Price Index for: United Kingdom. January 2007 to January 2014 (n.d.). Retrieved July 6, 2017, from http://landregistry.data.gov.uk/app/ukhpi/explore

The London economy was hot and the London real estate market was even hotter. Between 2007 and 2014, the average price of real estate in London increased from £267,658 to £355,830, a 32.9 percentage point appreciation, while the average price in the rest of England had risen over the same period from £181,124 to £188,265, a lowly 3.8 percentage point appreciation.

If one was already in the London real estate market, the values were appreciating. Getting into the market was comparatively more difficult for wage earners in London who were renting or for those outside of London entering the London market. While Americans were losing their homes in the Great Recession, home-owning Londoners realized noticeable contributions to their net worth because of rising home prices. Even with the importance of London as a financial hub, a look at the economic data leading up to the referendum suggests that there were serious cost of living and wage pressures for citizens in the United Kingdom. According to the OECD, between 2008 and 2013, Great Britain was among a handful of countries including Greece, the Czech Republic, Hungary, Portugal, Ireland and Italy that registered negative wage growth. The United Kingdom was a noticeable outlier to many of its neighbours and the OECD average. Average real wages in Great Britain had declined by 10 percent while the cost of living over a comparable period had increased by 22 percent. In effect, this represented a double hit – declining real wages combined with an increasing cost of living.

Figure 12
UK decline in real wages compared to cost of living
(Source: OECD data, Consumer Price Indices (CPIs) measure the average changes in the prices of consumer goods and services purchased by households.

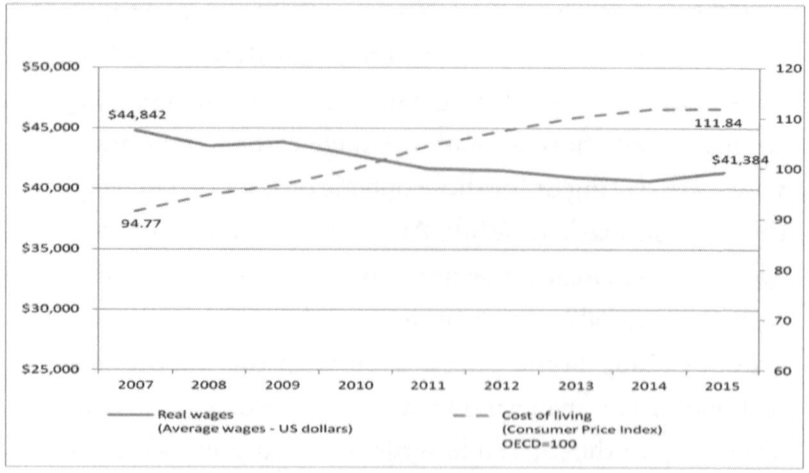

The key takeaway from the economic data is that there were citizens under significant financial pressure who likely felt they could just not get ahead. For those who lost their jobs, replacement jobs could be lower paying or part time. All this while the cost of living was going up. It was a similar story in the UK as the US. In the US, the anti-establishment anger was stoked by Trump telling Americans that both Washington and Wall Street were rigged and to blame, the nuance in England was that there were in effect two economies: the London knowledge economy and the rest of England. If you were in the London economy and a homeowner, you likely felt relatively comfortable about the future. If you were not part of the London financial hub you likely felt less comfortable. A look at the results of the Brexit vote suggest this 'two-state' mindset. The divide was not just between London and the rest of England; as in the United States, it was between voters with a higher educational attainment and those with a lower educational attainment.

A post-referendum analysis by the BBC of the voting in more than 1,000 local government wards suggests a high correlation between the profile of educational qualifications of voters and the vote outcome locally. The greater the number of individuals with a degree or an equivalent qualification, the higher the Remain vote, and the fewer individuals with a degree, the higher the Leave vote.

Figure 13
2016 UK Brexit Ward Vote by Education
(Source: BBC, Office for National Statistics, 1070 wards in England and Wales)

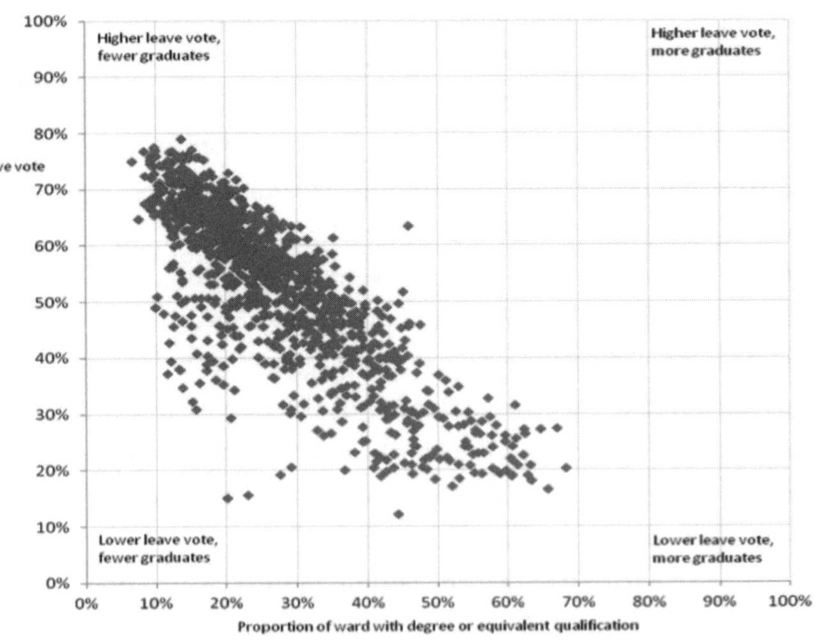

Source: Rosenbaum, M. (February 6, 2017). Local voting figures shed new light on EU referendum. Retrieved July 6, 2017, from http://www.bbc.com/news/uk-politics-38762034.

The mobilization of angry voters was more than a battle between the financial centre of Great Britain and the rest. It had an educational dimension. Voters without college or university education were more likely to find the Leave option appealing, believing that they had not benefited from the EU trade and labour-mobility relationship and that, as asserted by the Leave campaign and Farage, Great Britain was out of pocket to the tune of £350 million flowing out of the country to feed the Brussels EU establishment.

The numbers: The 'she loves me not – she loves me – she loves me not' trend line

Coming off his 2015 majority national election win, it looked for Prime Minister David Cameron that the mood to remain with the European Union was on the upswing. The trend line suggested that the Leave momentum was dissipating. Projecting out from the current trend pointed to a Remain victory if a referendum on the future of the relationship with the EU were called. But today's trend is only today's trend and not tomorrow's trend. A look at the compiled polling data suggests that the undecided markedly broke in favour of the Leave forces. In fact, a look at the trend-line in the close of the campaign indicates that the rise of Leave sentiment is a mirror image of the drop in undecided sentiment.

The narrative that the polling industry failed does not bear out the research. A number of the major pollsters, such as TNS and YouGov, which both projected a

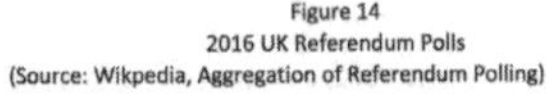

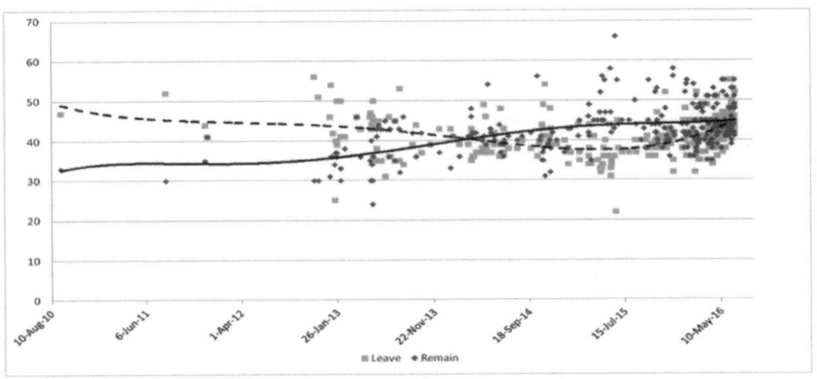

two percentage point victory for the Leave Campaign, had results close to the actual vote which was a 3.8 percentage point victory for the Leave Campaign. The losers in the estimation game were actually the bookmakers, who made Remain the odds-on favourite from the launch of the referendum even if they shortened the odds from an 82 percent chance to a 60 percent chance of the Remain side winning.[29] The challenge for casual observers is that one should not confuse the chance of an outcome with the actual outcome. It's similar to projecting the weather: A 60 percent chance of sunshine should not give one comfort that it will be a sunny day.

Out of 33.5 million votes cast in the 2015 UK Referendum, the Leave Campaign won by 1.2 million votes. In essence, a swing of one in 50 voters or 650,000 cast ballots from Leave to Remain would have yielded a different outcome. David Cameron would have had a near death

29 Lusher, A. (2016, June 21). EU referendum odds: Remain vote has always been bookies' favourite – and odds continue to shorten. Retrieved July 6, 2017, from http://www.independent.co.uk/news/uk/politics/eu-referendum-bookies-have-always-made-a-remain-vote-favourite-and-the-odds-continue-to-shorten-a7093971.html#commentsDiv.

political experience, remained as prime minister, and Great Britain would not have been immersed in discussions about exiting the European Union. Just as a point of context, in Canada the French-speaking province of Quebec had a referendum where the Yes forces (to stay in Canada) won by less than 50 thousand of 4.7 million votes – a margin of only one vote in 94. Another example of how the fragility of democracy means the future of nations can be decided by a handful of voters.

Former British prime minister Harold Macmillan, when asked what he feared most, responded, 'events, dear boy, events.'[30] Fast forward to the Internet age and it is not just events but the proliferation of opinion, information and misinformation. The coming of the Internet age for some heralded the hope of a new era for democracy. One where voters could be more engaged and better informed and where politicians who misrepresented the facts could be checked and chastised. After all, with the new World Wide Web, the truth would be at one's fingertips.

That big Leave campaign promise we made? Forget it. It was a mistake. It took about 60 minutes after the Leave campaign was declared the winner for it to climb down from its keynote message in the referendum. The assertion was that £350 million would be repatriated from the European Union and spent on the National Health Service in the wake of a Leave outcome. Boris Johnson, Michael Gove and Nigel Farage made the promise repeat-

30 Harris, R. (2002, June 4). As Macmillan never said: that's enough quotations. Retrieved July 6, 2017, from http://www.telegraph.co.uk/comment/personal-view/3577416/As-Macmillan-never-said-thats-enough-quotations.html.

edly during the referendum. The phrase 'We send the EU £350 million a week – let's fund our NHS instead – Vote Leave' adorned the side of the official Leave campaign bus.

The irony or tragedy, depending on one's view of the referendum results, is that voters were more likely to distrust what was likely the truth than what was later an abandoned promise and misleading political promise. An Ipsos MORI survey during the campaign suggested voters were suspicious of claims made by both the Leave and Remain campaigns. Almost one half of respondents (47 percent) surveyed just before the vote believed the false promise of the Leave campaign even though it was criticized by the UK Statistics Authority, while 70 percent of respondents in the same survey did not believe the treasury secretary's claim that households would be permanently worse off after Brexit.[31]

The question remains: Did the Leave forces know that the promise of funding the NHS instead of sending £350 million to the EU was incorrect, even in the face of criticism from the UK Statistics Authority? Realistically, one of two things occurred: They believed their numbers to be true or they knew there was an issue and refused to correct the mistake knowing it would damage their campaign. Regardless, the outcome was misinformation, unchecked, which in a very close race was believed by a

31 Stone, J. (2016, June 16). Nearly half of Britons believe Vote Leave's false '£350 million a week to the EU' claim. Retrieved July 6, 2017, from http://www.independent.co.uk/news/uk/politics/nearly-half-of-britons-believe-vote-leaves-false-350-million-a-week-to-the-eu-claim-a7085016.html.

significant proportion of voters[32]. The trend line over the course of the referendum suggested a shift of sentiment from undecided to the Leave camp. At best, this was an unfortunate occurrence in the campaign. At worst, this may have influenced enough citizens to tip the balance in favour of Brexit.

Although majorities of voters disbelieved both the Leave and the Remain assertions, the Brexit promises to repatriate the £350 million a week were more likely to be believed, even though they were proved to be based on incorrect information. In a referendum whose outcome would have changed with a swing of 1 in 50 voters, the veracity or lack of veracity of claims made by both sides is a significant contributor to the overall environment in which voters are trying to make decisions. Add to this a context of anger among voters who have seen their real wages decline over the past number of years, the movement of a relatively small group of voters in one direction or another, and one has a volatile situation in terms of outcome.

The economic call to arms by political outsider Nigel Farage was twinned with rhetoric about sovereignty and control of immigration. He opposed what he described as the open-door migration policy of the EU and asserted that a workforce already on its heels from declining wages would be further hit with waves of migrants

32 The Office for National Statistics published the 'UK Perspectives 2016: The UK contribution to the EU budget' release on 25 May 2016. This is available at http://visual.ons.gov.uk/uk-perspectives-2016-the-uk-contribution-to-the-eu-budget/ and sets out UK contributions to the EU budget.

entering the UK, migrants who had been let into Europe by the EU. Linking economic and xenophobic messages echoed Donald Trump's anti-trade anti-foreigner mantra. The reality is that even when racism is not widely held the rhetoric of nativist politicians is enabling and politically motivating for those who hold those racist minority opinions.

The politically wily Nigel Farage unexpectedly resigned as leader of UKIP very quickly on the heels of the Leave campaign victory, thus distancing himself from the controversial promise and also the fallout from the referendum vote. In a sense, he has escaped relatively unscathed as others grapple with the path forward for Great Britain. The referendum has elevated his celebrity-type status on the British and international political scene and has even garnered the attention of President Donald Trump, who likely saw the Brexit vote as yet another example of voters looking to punish failed systems. Farage, like Trump, was an outsider who fought hostile political and media establishments and won. Perhaps it should not have been a surprise that Farage was among the first international politicians to visit Trump and for Trump to muse that Farage would be a 'great UK ambassador to the US.'[33]

What can we learn from this? Start the angry voter fire, let it burn, then wait

Even though the Leave forces were a coalition, the per-

33 Woolf, N., & Elgot, J. (2016, November 22). Nigel Farage would be great UK ambassador to US, says Donald Trump. Retrieved July 6, 2017, from https://www.theguardian.com/politics/2016/nov/22/nigel-farage-uk-ambassador-us-donald-trump.

sonality and style of Nigel Farage loomed large in the campaign. He was both provocateur and outsider. In a country where real wages had noticeably declined, he was the anti-establishment symbol, and singled out the British establishment and European Union as problems. Both populist and demagogue, he was one of the key leaders of the Leave forces that effectively played on the emotions of citizens.

For many outside observers, the outcome of the 2016 UK referendum as to whether the United Kingdom should stay or leave the European Union was a head scratcher. One would expect that given the advantages the Cameron Conservatives had of controlling the timing, the question and the opening environment of the campaign, the outcome should have been a foregone conclusion favouring the Remain outcome. The pro-European Union Cameron forces misunderstood an electorate hammered by a drop in real wages and tired of European politics. England was, de facto, two countries – one country being the pro-European capital in London which had benefitted from and prospered under the Union and the other country being the rest of the UK, which emerged more of a prosperity spectator than a prosperity participant. Likewise, the anti-establishment guise of the Leave forces played on a dislike of EU bureaucrats and migrant workers, and resonated well with voters who had a lower educational attainment.

While the pro-Europe forces sought to engage in a debate and advance rational arguments about policy choices and the value of the European Union, the Brexiteers, led by Nigel Farage, rode to victory on anger yearning to judge the establishment, irrespective of the potential negative consequences of a UK departure from the European Union. The lesson is that citizens in the UK saw the vote as a referendum not only on the EU but on the UK establishment and that voters, traditionally more risk averse on economic issues, were willing to risk sending a message to Whitehall, the seat of the British central government. This is the punishment dimension of the new age of voter rage.

DEBT
Europ
rm
JUNE 8
2017
EU
Election
Home Office
Great Britain
Theresa
Tory
Corbyn
May
Jeremy
SNP
BREXIT
Sta
opposition
UKIP
Labour
steady
Tim farron
Party

MANY NOT THE FEW

CHAPTER 4

I'd Like my Election Shaken, Not Stirred: How the Age Margins Squeezed the May Tories

They said she was unbeatable. Sitting on a whopping 21-point advantage over the United Kingdom's Labour Party, according to some pollsters, Theresa May looked poised to win upwards of a very comfortable 100-seat majority victory. After all, voters seemed satisfied with her firm handling of Brexit, the Labour Party caucus was in disarray, and Labour Party Leader Jeremy Corbyn's personal numbers were in the doldrums. Then, something peculiar happened—an election. In a world where small swings have a big impact on the electoral outcomes and where voters are increasingly looking for a political target on which to vent their frustration with the system, Theresa May's victory somehow went from a sure-thing to a toss-up.

It started with an odd election call. Theoretically, the Fixed-term Parliaments Act 2011[34] puts the power

34 General elections. (n.d.). Retrieved July 6, 2017, from http://www.parliament.uk/about/how/elections-and-voting/general/.

Figure 15

Pasokification – The hollowing out of a governing party

(Source: Hellenic Republic Elections, 2009-2015)

	October 4th, 2009 Election Results (%)	May 6th, 2012 Election Results (%)	June 17th, 2012 Election Results (%)	January 25th, 2015 Election Results (%)	September 20, 2015 Election Results (%)
Panhellenic Social Movement (PASOK)	43.9	13.2	12.3	4.7	6.3
New Democracy (ND)	33.5	18.9	29.7	27.8	28.1
Communist Party of Greece (KKE)	7.5	8.5	4.5	5.5	5.6
Coalition of the Radical Left (SYRIZA)	4.6	16.8	26.9	36.3	35.5
Popular Association-Golden Dawn (XA)	-	7.0	6.9	6.3	7.0
The River (Potami)	-	-	-	6.0	4.1
Independent Greeks (ANEL)	-	10.6	7.5	4.8	3.7

Source: General Election Results, Hellenic Republic, 2009 to 2015, http://electionresources.org/gr

to call the election in the hands of Parliament, not the prime minister. Traditionally, the governing party in the House of Commons, led by the prime minister, calls and shapes the timing of general elections. The act, introduced during the coalition government between the Cameron Conservatives and Nick Clegg's Liberal Democrats, fixed general election dates every five years, starting in 2015, 2020, 2025 and so forth, but also allowed for elections outside of the set cycle with two-thirds support of the House of Commons. What was odd was the support of Labour MPs for a Conservative snap election motion when the polling suggested a likely win for the Tories and a very likely big loss for Labour. In that respect, the support for the motion laid bare the Labour caucus' desire to turf its own leader. For some Labour members of Parliament, Corbyn was too socialist, too strident and unelectable. From their perspective, this was the opportunity to instigate an election-driven coup d'état of the Labour Party leadership. If Labour had no chance to win, then this was the opportunity to get rid of Corbyn and start the party renewal process.

With the Conservatives trending upward in the polls and preparing for the Brexit negotiations, it wasn't surprising that May wanted to strengthen her parliamentary majority which would also, by extension, strengthen Her negotiating position with the European Union in June 2017. For May and the Conservatives, it was a smash and grab strong majority strategy. For some Labour MPs, it was merely a smash strategy with the hope that Corbyn would be the victim.

Neither strategy was successful. Corbyn and Labour nearly snatched victory and May's Conservatives lost their party majority and were forced to ally with the surly DUP in Northern Ireland to stay in power. In that sense, the Conservative government was shaken. Even with the supposed 21-point advantage in the polls on day one of the campaign, there were a number of indicators that suggested that the May advantage was more a Potemkin village, which Corbyn eventually exposed with much help from the Conservative campaign itself.

What Corbyn learned from the Greeks

Labour strives to be a big-tent party. In the modern era it, along with the Conservative Party, is one of the two major parties that traditionally govern the United Kingdom. Labour grew out of a trade union movement but includes more moderate voices such as those that rallied around former Labour Prime Minister Tony Blair, who tilted the party to being more centrist on many issues. One of the manifestations of this new age of voter rage is the further polarization of voters and parties. Although the polarization has been striking in the United States, it has also occurred in other democracies. Greece, for example, was up until 2015 generally governed by two major parties, the center right Nea Dimoktratia, or New Democracy Party, and the center left PASOK. During the Greek debt crisis, the PASOK center left party which in 2009 won the election with 44 percent support saw its support drop to five percent. This drop coincided with the rise of the far-left Syriza Party. In the short span of six years, the once-mighty PASOK, which was the moderate progressive party, went from being the government to being decimated in favour of a more extreme left-wing party. This phenomenon is now referred to as Pasokification, as moderate left-wing parties are on the decline not just in Greece but across Europe.[35]

As sub-sets of voters become increasingly disillusioned with the system and anti-establishment in perspective, establishment parties are on their heels because they are perceived as agents of the establishment. In this environment, voters are turning towards either party outsiders (Trump and Sanders in the US) or outside parties (such as Macron's En Marche! in France) to voice their disapproval and vent their electoral rage. Corbyn's left-wing policies, although anathema to the London elites, remade the Labour Party from an establishment style party to an

35 Rose thou art sick. (2016, April 2). The Economist Magazine. Retrieved July 6, 2017, from http://www.economist.com/news/briefing/21695887-centre-left-sharp-decline-across-europe-rose-thou-art-sick.

outside party. The '#wedemand' campaign, built on the Labour policy manifesto, was a direct shot over the bow of the political establishment and elites and predicated on the demand for a 'fairer society, run in the interests of the many, not the few.'[36] With a decline in real wages leading up to the Brexit vote, the idea that something was wrong, that the system was rigged, rang as authentic for many voters. Labour tapped into the sentiment driven by the unemployed, the underemployed, struggling workers and those who saw prosperity as something for others to enjoy. In that sense, the election became a referendum on the Theresa May Conservatives and second referendum on Brexit. Corbyn tapped into a new popular front which was an amalgam of margins and the marginalized: the margins being those in the workforce struggling to make ends meet, and the marginalized being those pro-European young voters whose views were marginalized in the Brexit vote outcome. In the 2017 UK general election, these groups were back and ready to make a statement. Theresa May's advantage in the public opinion polls was masked by a high level of anxiety and potential volatility.

The trajectory of public opinion

For argument's sake, the three most common trends in public opinion data are: the straight line where public opinion seems unchanged or steady, the downward trajectory, or the upward trajectory. Straight trend lines in public opinion are like holding patterns where the status

36 Corbyn, J. (2017, June 2). #WeDemand. Official Jeremy Corbyn Channel, YouTube. Retrieved July 6, 2017, from https://www.youtube.com/watch?v=28-fC6_ByuO.

quo reigns until an event occurs to move the numbers. When the trajectory moves either up or down, the key characteristics to look at are the angle of the public opinion trajectory and the margin between first and second place. The trend lines can narrow or widen, or it can be a steep cliff-like drop or spike. Alternatively, it can be a steady withering-on-the-vine type decline or steady growth in support. The other thing to look at is whether the trend is normal or exceptional. A ballot advantage in the polls of anywhere from zero to 10 percent could be seen as normal depending on the context. Massive advantages should be seen as exceptional circumstances waiting for a technical correction.

A public opinion technical correction is similar to a technical correction in the stock market. In the stock market, a technical correction can occur when there is no fundamental reason[37] for the change (such as a dividend or earnings statement). It is about investors being cautious and thinking that the stock is overvalued, thus driving prices down. In that sense, the Conservative advantage was ripe for a technical correction. The May Conservatives certainly had an advantage but their political capital was overpriced. More importantly, in these circumstances there is significant voter volatility beneath the surface. When a party enjoys an exceptional lead in the polls, the last voters joining the bandwagon are usually softer voters and are vulnerable to swinging away from the current choice.

---

37 Investopedia Staff. (2007, June 5). Technical Correction. Retrieved July 6, 2017, from http://www.investopedia.com/terms/t/technical_correction.asp.

What was clear from a numbers perspective is that the margin for Conservative support, when it stood at an exceptional advantage, could only narrow. The only uncertainty was how much. The Conservative trend line declined over time while support for Labour increased at the cost of the Conservatives and lesser parties.

Figure 16
UK General Election Tracking – April 18 to June 8, 2017
(Source: Poll Aggregation, Wikipedia)

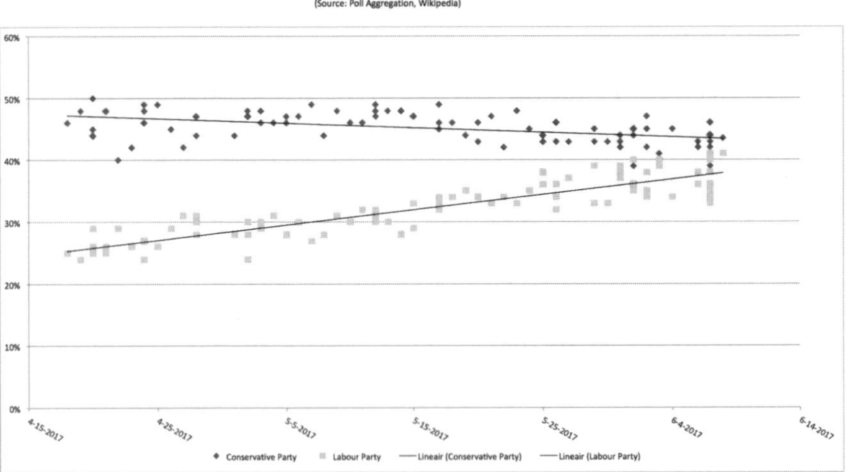

The other factor that was not 'priced' into the Conservative support in the polling data prior to the election was the structure of non-election and election media coverage. In non-election cycles, governing parties enjoy a structural advantage when it comes to media coverage. The leader of the government of the day is the default focus of the media. By merely governing, introducing legislation, responding to the happenings in the nation and abroad, Theresa May, as prime minister, naturally had by default a disproportionate profile and share of media attention compared to Jeremy Corbyn. In these circumstances, opposition parties do not get as much profile and have more of a 'me too' role. However, when the election is called, a different media coverage dynamic kicks in. In the non-election cycle, it is mostly about the big issues that face the nation and what citizens should be concerned about. During an election campaign, the media either formally or informally shift to have more and balanced coverage of all the major parties contending in the election. From the day the writs were issued for the campaign, May had to share the spotlight. Corbyn, who had to fight for coverage in the non-election cycle, now had a platform for his attacks on the government.

In terms of trajectory for the Conservatives, the public opinion trend line could only be negative because it was exceptionally high and in an election cycle their incumbency advantage for media coverage would also not be as strong. The 21-point advantage purported in the media vanished into a two-percentage point win on election day. The swing of a mere one in 50 voters away from the Conservatives would have resulted in outsider Jeremy Corbyn and his Labour Party occupying 10 Downing Street as the government. The election had gone from romp to rout. The irony of the outcome is that, while it was the result of Labour running a solid campaign, connecting into voter anxiety, positioning itself as a party outside of the establishment, it was assisted by the unforced errors of the Conservative Party.

'Events, dear boy, events': How the UK Conservatives nearly toppled themselves

Attributed to Conservative Prime Minister Harold Macmillan[38], the quotation about 'events' reminds us that public opinion is fragile and influenced by outside shocks. For an incumbent, the ideal campaign can be the 'Seinfeld election', an election about nothing. These sorts of elections tend to favour incumbents. There is no burning desire for change. Voter turnout is low. The alternatives to the governing party are not compelling and there are no flash points. Lacking fire, tension or the desire for change, the status quo going into an election usually prevails. For the May Conservatives, the ideal campaign would be one where Theresa May was confirmed as prime minister with her own mandate and things would continue at Whitehall after the election, business as usual. Corbyn would be dismissed as a radical and unstable governing alternative to May, and voters would see the need for a strong Conservative May-led mandate to negotiate the Brexit they had asked for in the referendum.

It was not to be. Although the media's duty to provide balanced coverage creates a daily grind of quips, attacks and counter-attacks, the media's business imperative is to engage voters and grab the attention of viewers and readers. Elections are usually a horse race or a car crash. Both can be good at engaging voters. The 2017 UK general election was both a car crash and a horse race.

38 Oxford Reference. (2016, March 15). Retrieved July 6, 2017, from http://www.oxfordreference.com/view/10.1093/acref/9780199916108.001.0001/acref-9780199916108-e-2597.

For the Conservatives, it seemed rather innocuous. In the Tory manifesto was a proposal to increase the income means test for seniors' home care from £23,250 to £100,000 with payments for home care being deferred until after life by one's estate.[39] The key challenge was including the home of a senior as a source of funds for either residential or domiciliary care.[40] Labour asserted that this would result in a significant extra financial burden as estates and people's homes would need to be liquidated to cover bills for seniors' care. Corbyn and the Labour Party were quick to characterize the initiative as a 'dementia tax' because it would result in a disparity between seniors who were cancer sufferers and likely required shorter seniors' home care compared to seniors with Alzheimer's who might need longer home care and thus potentially bear a greater financial burden.

A political furore erupted. Conservative support, especially among seniors, who were a key demographic driving Tory fortunes, plummeted and the Tories did a policy U-turn. According to *The Telegraph*, 'Mrs. May became the first prime minister in living memory to change a manifesto pledge before an election when she announced there would be a cap on the amount pensioners will have to pay.'[41] This was the political equiv-

39 Conservative Government. (n.d.). Forward Together, The Conservative and Unionist Party Manifesto 2017 (p. 67). https://s3.eu-west-2.amazonaws.com/manifesto2017/Manifesto2017.pdf#page=67.

40 Domiciliary Care. (n.d.). Retrieved July 6, 2017, from http://www.northerntrust.hscni.net/services/352.htm. Domiciliary care includes help with personal care and other practical household tasks. This compares to residential care which is in a seniors residence.

41 Hughes, L. (2017, May 29). Families could see up to half the value of their home put at risk under 'dementia tax'. The Telegraph. Retrieved July 6, 2017, from http://www.telegraph.co.uk/news/2017/05/28/families-could-see-half-value-home-put-risk-dementia-tax/.

alent of an own-goal, with the Tories shooting the ball into their own net. In one quick motion, the Conservatives repelled a core supporter group (seniors), ceded the definition of their initiative as a 'dementia tax' and had the sitting prime minister reverse on a policy issue mid-campaign. The insurmountable lead reported by the media was now in jeopardy.

On May 22nd, 2017, there was a tragic terror attack in Manchester during the election campaign. At a concert of American pop singer Ariana Grande, a British citizen detonated a homemade bomb and killed 22 people, including children.[42] On June 3rd, days before the election vote, another attack in London Bridge also took the lives of eight people.[43] Tragic events such as terror attacks are a time for community and national unity. Setting aside the common sense of purpose and solidarity of citizens and politicians from across the United Kingdom in response to the terror attacks, they did cast a light on the prime minister's track record as home secretary under the previous prime minister, David Cameron. The home secretary is responsible for the internal affairs of England and Wales, including policing. Under May's watch, Whitehall cut funding for police budgets by 20 percent.[44] Although terror attacks are often opportunities for politicians to lead a nation, in this particular case, very close

42 Manchester attack: Who were the victims? (2017, June 03). BBC News. Retrieved July 6, 2017, from http://www.bbc.com/news/uk-40012738.
43 Davies, C. (2017, June 7). London Bridge attack: last of eight victims identified as Xavier Thomas. The Guardian. Retrieved July 6, 2017, from https://www.theguardian.com/uk-news/2017/jun/07/london-bridge-attack-last-of-eight-victims-identified-as-xavier-thomas.
44 Travis, A. (2016, July 18). What does Theresa May's record as home secretary tell us? The Guardian. Retrieved July 6, 2017, from https://www.theguardian.com/politics/2016/jul/18/what-does-theresa-mays-record-as-home-secretary-tell-us.

to the election vote, the conversation focused on May's cuts to police and their implications for national security.

By the time of the second terror attack and in the wake of the dementia tax debacle, the narrative of the campaign had decidedly shifted. The Conservatives, once confident in victory and expecting a resounding new majority mandate, were battling for their very survival in the closing days of the election. May had done a major policy U-turn, didn't show up for the leaders' debates and had to defend her record of cutting police budgets. All the while, Corbyn and Labour were railing against the establishment elites embodied by May and the Conservatives, and were mobilizing those in the margins, the underemployed and the young who rejected Brexit and the old who were repelled by the dementia tax. This unlikely coalition was intent on toppling the Conservatives.

How age margins nearly toppled Theresa May

Politics and elections are messy. Neat and tidy explanations might give some comfort and make for quick short-form conclusions, but when one digs beneath the top numbers certain complexities and levels of nuance emerge. If voters are not homogenous in their backgrounds and views, why should we expect the explanation of elections to be so? A number of observers have distilled the outcome of the UK election as accountable to the rising up of young voters, and saw the 2017 UK election as an all-out generational war between the youthful and mobile Remain forces and the more senior and fixed Brexiteers. The political ledger for change, in that view, was firmly divided between the young and old, with the young fighting the Conservative establishment and the old defending it.

A look at the research data conducted by Survation, which by most measures had a very good estimate of the popular vote in the 2017 UK general election[45], suggests a number of key observations that debunk some of the myths about the 2017 election.

First, although the aggregation of data from all the pollsters suggested a 21-point advantage for Theresa May and the Conservatives at the call of the election, the one outlier in terms of the scope of the Conservative advantage was Survation. Their first survey, completed April 21, 2017, after the call of the election on April 18, suggested that the Conservatives enjoyed a more modest but still strong 11-point lead over Labour, with the Conservatives registering 40 percent support to Labour's 29 percent support.[46] Most of the major pollsters in the UK underestimated support for Labour in their final call with estimates ranging from a low of 34 percent to a high of 40 percent (Survation). This suggests that the modeling conducted by a number of pollsters, a number of whom had re-estimated who would likely vote because of their referendum mis-predictions for the 2017 general election, adjusted their estimates in ways that consistently underrepresented the support of Labour throughout the

45 The final voter prediction for Survation was 41 percent Conservative to 40 percent Labour (a one point margin for the Tories), with the election result being 43.5 percent Conservative to 41 percent Labour (a two-and-a-half point margin for the Tories).

46 General election 2017 poll. (2017, April 22). Retrieved July 6, 2017, from http://survation.com/wp-content/uploads/2017/04/MOS-GE-Tables-I-2c0d7h2-2004SWCH.pdf.

election. The Survation polling at the beginning of the campaign pointed to a comfortable Conservative win, but not of the huge proportion estimated by most of the other pollsters. If the Survation polling was closer to capturing the reality, then the media and pundit narrative of a massive Conservative victory was effectively a fiction – the Conservatives were strong, but not as strong as many believed.

Second, the campaign was, for some, a quasi-replay of the European Union referendum and a chance to send a message to Theresa May's Conservatives. As Labour closed the gap with the Tories, it became clear to some voters that Labour was the primary vehicle to send a message to Whitehall, which was signaling a hard Brexit stance for the upcoming negotiations with the European Union. The Survation data of voting preferences tabulated by the past vote on the EU referendum suggests that Remain sentiment increasingly coalesced around Labour. At the beginning of the campaign, 38 percent of Remain voters supported Labour, 29 percent supported the Conservatives and 17 percent the Liberal Democrats. By the close of the campaign, among Remain voters, Labour had shot up from 38 to 54 percent support while the Liberal Democrats had dropped to 11 percent support. Among the voter movements in the election, Labour became the parking place for Remain voters disenchanted with the impending Brexit as the key challenger to May's Conservatives.

Third, a dominant post-election narrative to explain the crumbling of Tory fortunes was the generational rift between young voters and seniors. Young people wanted to remain in the European Union. They were angry over the referendum outcome and the path towards Brexit. They came out, voted and almost toppled the May government. This was the simple black-and-white explanation of the outcome. Digging into the numbers suggests that the May Conservatives were caught in a demographic vice grip between both young voters and seniors. This was not a phenomenon of the rage of the young (the 'youthquake') but of the young and the old.

According to Survation (see Figure 17 below), the Conservatives enjoyed a whopping 33-percentage point advantage over Labour among voters 55 years of age and older, had no perceptible advantage among middle aged voters and trailed Labour by 14 points among voters under 35 years of age. By the end of the campaign, the Labour advantage among younger voters ramped up to 29 points and the Conservative advantage of older voters dropped nine points. The 29-point gap in support between Labour and the Conservatives among younger voters in the close of the election is the basis for the youth narrative in the media. This dramatic Labour advantage and shift is clear but it does not factor in the true proportion of likely young, middle aged and senior voters. A look at the polling data that adds the lens of political muscle (i.e., who comes out to vote) suggests that seniors had as much if not more of an impact on the outcome of the election than young voters in terms of positively driving Labour.

Figure 17
2017 UK General Election - Absolute Impact of Vote Swings
(Source: Survation Election Polling, April 22, 2017 and June 7, 2017)

		Age			
		18-34	35-54	55+	Total
Election End June 7 Polling	Conservative Support	26.5%	40.9%	52.5%	41.5%
	Labour Support	55.1%	41.9%	28.8%	40.4%
	Conservative Advantage	-29	-1	24	1
Election Start April 22 Polling	Conservative Support	24.8%	31.4%	54.4%	39.6%
	Labour Support	38.5%	30.5%	21.7%	28.6%
	Conservative Advantage	-14	1	33	11
	Change in Conservative Advantage	-15	-2	-9	
	Percentage of Likely Voters	23.9%	33.7%	42.4%	
	Absolute Impact (Advantage multiplied by Likely Voters times 10)	-35	-6	-38	

Source: Survation, http://survation.com/archive/2017-2/

Survation estimates of likely voters suggested that 23.9 percent of voters would be under 35 years of age, 33.7 percent would be middle aged, and 42.4 percent would be 55 years of age and older. Although the most dramatic margin and change occurred among younger voters, in absolute terms – that is, in terms of voting muscle (citizens who actually vote) – they represent a minority of voters: less than one in four, according to Survation's last survey prior to voting day. Taking the voter swings in opinion and mapping them over who the likely voters are suggests that the swing of seniors away from the Conservatives, although not as dramatic as the youth swing, had as much or more of a true impact on Conservative and Labour Party fortunes than young voters. In this case, multiplying the proportion of the electorate by the swing indicates that it was the two tails of the demographic margins that turned the election against the Conservatives. All this while middle aged voters were divided at the beginning and the end of the election. The rage of voters in the 2017 UK Election had two angry tails: the youthful anti-Brexit voters; and the seniors scared by the Conservative dementia tax issue.

Figure 18
2017 UK General Election: The Two Angry Tails
(Source: Survation, Election Polling, April 22, 2017 and June 7, 2017)

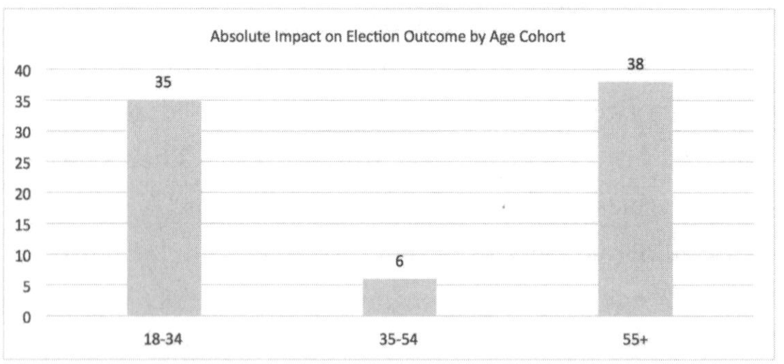

What lessons can we take away from the UK's 2017 general election?

The lessons from the UK election are many. First, a review of the research data suggests that the magnitude of the Conservative advantage going into the election may have been overstated and fed a media narrative of a seemingly inevitable and massive Conservative win, which was misplaced. Second, even with the Conservative advantage, the structure of the campaign – that is, the need to have balanced coverage between parties – meant that the trajectory of the Conservative trend line was likely to always be negative, with the one big unknown being how steep that negative trajectory might be as the political marketplace repriced the true strength of the Tories over the course of the campaign. Third, Labour benefited from a coalescing of Remain sentiment behind Jeremy Corbyn. Finally but most importantly, the one-two punch of disgruntled young voters and concerned seniors led to the near toppling of the May Tory government.

What is interesting about the UK election is that the rage was driven by different factors but rallied behind one primary choice: Labour. The young were angry about Brexit and seniors were concerned about the dementia tax. Together they shook up the Theresa May Conservatives and nearly catapulted radical outsider Jeremy Corbyn into 10 Downing Street. The near-upset occurred even though, counter to popular wisdom, Corbyn has steered his Labour Party manifesto decidedly to the left with a tone of radicalism and anti-establishment resistance. In this case, seniors who are usually more conservative joined the angry voters on the margin and tilted the balance.

CHAPTER 5
L'État, C'est Moi[47]: How a Rothschild Banker Smashed France's Party System

He was too young, a socialist, a banker, and a self-styled anti-establishment maverick. Finding himself without a party, he created his own – En Marche! – roughly translated as 'On the Move!' (don't forget the exclamation point). In November 2016, Emmanuel Macron launched his new party and his campaign for president of France and within a mere six months was elected president and smashed France's party system in the process. His movement and meteoric rise were a result of a number of factors, including the polarization of politics in France to the right and to the left, the tribulations of his opponents and the underlying economic anxiety that still grips France. Regardless, he singlehandedly created a new political movement and through the sheer force of his vision and personality won the French presidency. In that respect,

47 'I am the state': a quote attributed to King Louis XIV of France.

the post-victory Macron became the embodiment of the French state – l'état, c'est Macron.

For some, though, his victory was a sigh of relief against the populist politics of the likes of Marine Le Pen, the reality is that the first round of the French presidential race was quite close. Macron's overwhelming win in the second round and parliamentary elections mask a country still polarized with the margins and the marginalized gaining strength. The Macron win is more a political down payment on the future of France than a settling into a new wave of post-populist stability. Underlying stresses related to high unemployment rates in France persist and the extremes have gained in strength, even though they did not win.

To an outsider, it might have seemed odd. Macron had just won the second round of the French presidential election with 66 percent to Le Pen's 34 percent – a margin of 32 points, yet his acceptance speech spoke of divisions. Picture a US presidential race where one candidate won by 32 points in a two-person race and then went on to talk about healing the divisions in America – it's hard to imagine. For Macron in France, that is the case. Even with his very comfortable victory, on election night he promised the French nation, 'I will do everything to make sure you never have reason again to vote for extremes.'[48] The data suggests that if less than one in 20 French voters had moved away from Macron to any of the other front run-

48 Chrisafis, A. (2017, May 8). Emmanuel Macron vows unity after winning French presidential election. The Guardian. Retrieved July 6, 2017, from https://www.theguardian.com/world/2017/may/07/emmanuel-macron-wins-french-presidency-marine-le-pen.

ners in the first round of the presidential run-off, Macron might have been a footnote in French political history. His win was propelled by his personal charisma and vision, his strategic positioning as an agent of change, and a heavy dose of political serendipity, much of which was provided by his opponents.

The odd intersection of a dwarf toss, a Rothschild banker, nepotism and voter anger

Although French politics has never lacked for excitement, the combination of front runners in the 2017 presidential race merits some focus. The race featured the two ideological extremes, one centrist conservative and Macron, the former Socialist Party member now independently positioned as neither right nor left. On the extremes were Marine Le Pen, head of the right-wing Front National (FN), and Jean-Luc Mélenchon, a former Socialist Party member leading the left wing movement La France Insoumise (Unbowed France). François Fillon led the conservative Les Républicains and Emmanuel Macron led En Marche!

From left wing to right wing, the top contenders to be president of France reflect the divisions and tensions in the country. On the far left, Communist-backed Jean-Luc Mélenchon led La France Insoumise (Unbowed France). Born in Tangier, Morocco, and of humble beginnings, he is an ideological thinker and prolific political writer of the left. Disappointed with France's Socialist Party becoming too mainstream for his liking, his Unbowed France movement was created to recapture leftist zeal. He believes in a bottom-up citizens' revolution in France, embodied in the Movement for the Sixth Republic (M6R)[49] which is influenced by his new focus on ecological politics and revolutions in Latin America and the Arab Spring. His 350-point manifesto, La Force du Peuple (the Force of the People), included wide ranging promises including a 100-percent tax on the rich, getting out of the North Atlantic Treaty Organization (NATO), investing €100 billion into green projects while getting out of nuclear power generation, reducing the work week to 32 hours and reinstating full retirement to 60 years of age.[50] An avid walker and without a driver's license, Mélenchon has firm views on society. During an interview in 2013[51] he recalled the story of a game in a night club in his constituency, 'throwing the dwarf', which he asked be banned. According to Mélenchon, the dwarf who was the main attraction in the night club game self-declared as being happy to be tossed, was glad to earn a living, to get attention and to have the star status that came with the game. Even though the dwarf asserted it was none of Mélenchon's business how one made a living, Mélenchon asked that the game be banned because he did not want to live in a society where something like this takes place.

49 Flenady, L. (2015, January 12). Welcome to 'The Era of the People': Jean-Luc Mélenchon Envisions a Citizens' Revolution. Occupy.com. Retrieved July 6, 2017, from http://www.occupy.com/article/welcome-era-people-jean-luc-m%C3%A9lenchon-envisions-citizens-revolution#sthash.2C1iPO4i.dpbs.

50 Rejoindre la France Insoumise. (n.d.). Retrieved July 6, 2017, from https://lafranceinsoumise.fr/.

51 Bechler, R. (2013, January 11). Open Democracy. France is a universal nation: Mélenchon speaks out. Retrieved July 6, 2017, from https://www.opendemocracy.net/rosemary-bechler/jean-luc-melenchon-interview.

The Mélenchon world is one of principle and ideology. He works to live his manifesto and is quick to intervene on behalf of his personal vision of right, wrong and how things should be.

Then there was former Socialist cabinet minister Emmanuel Macron, who was the youngest candidate in the race, and as the winner is France's youngest-ever president at 39 years of age. An accomplished pianist and practicing kick-boxer[52], Macron was a gifted student by all accounts. He met his wife, Brigitte Trogneaux, a French teacher, as her 17-year-old student. She is 24 years his senior and his life and political partner. He is a graduate of the prestigious Lycée Henri-IV in Paris, has a master's degree in public affairs from Sciences Po, and also attended the École National d'Administration which is the training ground for leading civil servants in France. Macron also worked as an investment banker with Rothschild & Co.[53] After serving in Socialist Party Prime Minister François Hollande's cabinet as minister of the economy, he formed his new movement En Marche! intent on fighting the politics of the extremes as embodied by leaders like Le Pen and Mélenchon. Neither right nor left, according to Macron, En Marche! is intended to mobilize and unify a divided France. Many assert his style of politics is similar to the 'third way' as embodied by politicians like Democrat President Bill Clinton in the

52 Willsher, K. (2016, April 10). Emmanuel Macron: France's political prince eyeing the Elysée | Observer profile. The Guardian. Retrieved July 6, 2017, from https://www.theguardian.com world/2016/apr/10/emmanuel-macron-france-president.

53 Ott, T. (2017, May 15). Emmanuel Macron. Biography Website. Retrieved July 6, 2017, from https://www.biography.com/people/emmanuel-macron-050817.

United States and Labour Prime Minister Tony Blair in the United Kingdom. The 'third way' is seen by some as a centrist solution to increasingly polarized left-wing and right-wing political dialogue. Macron's presidential platform included €50 billion in public investment, spending cuts, tax changes for lower-income individuals and investors, and a liberalized labour market.[54] Described by many as a maverick, he has had an unconventional career path being both a Socialist cabinet minister and an investment banker and has, for some, an unconventional marriage because of the age difference. Having created his movement on the sheer force of his personality and vision for France, Macron has the trappings of the establishment elite in his profile but acts like an outsider.

François Fillon, on the centre right, was prime minister of France under President Nicholas Sarkozy and by all accounts at the onset should have been a heavy favourite in the race for the French presidency. He was the nominee for Les Républicains (LR), a center-right conservative political party in France and defeated, in a surprising outcome, his former political boss Sarkozy in the party primary. A conservative and a Catholic, he has a graduate degree in public law and has had a long political career wherein he has served in a diversity of cabinet positions in the French government. He is a fan of General Charles de Gaulle and Margaret Thatcher. His wife, Penelope, is Welsh. It was a focus on payments to his wife that helped scuttle his bid for the French presi-

54 Briançon, P. (2017, February 27). Emmanuel Macron splits baby with campaign platform. Politico. Retrieved July 6, 2017, from http://www.politico.eu/article/emmanuel-macron-platform-news-election-analysis-france-reforms/.

dency. Known by some as 'Penelopegate', the controversy surrounded payments of about €800,000 to his wife out of parliamentary funds.[55] It is a well-known practice, and not illegal, for parliamentarians to have family members on staff. According to the investigative website Mediapart, '52 wives, 28 sons and 32 daughters of deputies' were employed using parliamentary funds in 2014 with at least 20 percent of members of Parliament paying a member of their immediate family.[56] The issue for Fillon was conflicting accounts as to whether his wife had shown up for work. This issue did not reconcile well with his platform to launch a new austerity plan for France which included cutting public spending and reducing the size of government. Fillon was in favour of a quick Brexit, wanted to lay off up 500,000 state workers to fund corporate tax breaks, opposed gay marriage and favoured better relations with Russia to help protect Christians in the Middle East.[57] Within a broader environment where voters are skeptical of politicians, charges of nepotism cut to the heart of his chances to become president of France.

Rounding out the top contenders was Marine Le Pen. Le Pen leads the right-wing National Front (FN). She is the softer, more media savvy successor to her father Jean-Marie Le Pen, whom many considered xeno-

55 Chassany, A. (2017, February 2). Fillon's Fall from Grace. The Financial Times. Retrieved July 6, 2017, from https://www.ft.com/content/d6bff950-e7d1-11e6-967b-c88452263daf.
56 Mathieu, M. (2014, July 27). L'Assemblée a rémunéré 52 épouses, 28 fils et 32 filles de députés en 2014. Mediapart. Retrieved July 6, 2017, from https://www.mediapart.fr/journal/france/270714/lassemblee-remunere-52-epouses-28-fils-et-32-filles-de-deputes-en-2014?onglet=full.
57 Telegraph Reporters. (2017, April 23). Who is Francois Fillon and why is he being investigated? The Telegraph. Retrieved July 6, 2017, from http://www.telegraph.co.uk/news/0/francois-fillon-investigated/.

phobic and anti-Semitic and who also led France's right-wing National Front party. In her views, she has been more anti-Clinton than pro-Trump, but has been cordial with the new Trump administration. Because of her life story which included obtaining a master of laws degree and a master of advance studies degree in criminal law[58], and her political lineage, one would think that it would be hard for her to portray herself as a political outsider. Le Pen's strategy, similar to Trump's and Farage's, was to run against the establishment, globalization and immigrants. She attacked 'savage globalization', which she claims is personified by Macron as the investment banker. Whereas Macron defended the humanitarian welcoming of Syrian refugees in Europe, Le Pen advanced a platform which gave priority to French people over non-nationals in jobs, housing and welfare.[59] Le Pen's form of extremism of the right was perceived by many as the key threat in the presidential election.

As Macron emerged as a key challenger, more moderate forces rallied to his candidacy to block Le Pen. Leading centrist and president of the moderate Democratic Movement François Bayrou endorsed Macron, as did a number of socialist, centrist and centre-right members of Parliament[60]. A popular front against the extremes was forming in the second round. And it should be no

58 Ray, M. (n.d.). Marine Le Pen. Britannica. Retrieved July 6, 2017, from https://www.britannica.com/biography/Marine-Le-Pen.

59 Chrisafis, A. (2017, April 24). Marine Le Pen rails against rampant globalisation after election success. The Guardian. Retrieved July 6, 2017, from https://www.theguardian.com/world/2017/apr/24/marine-le-pen-rails-against-rampant-globalisation-after-election-success.

60 Le Monde.fr. (2017, March 21). Qui sont les soutiens du candidat Macron? Le Monde. Retrieved July 6, 2017, from http://www.lemonde.fr/election-presidentielle-2017/article/2017/02/28/les-soutiens-d-emmanuel-macron_5087064_4854003.html.

surprise because the first round showed a tight four-way race with a good showing for both the right-wing and the left-wing parties.

Was it really a landslide? How a 1-in-20 swing would have changed the race for president

A look at the outcome of the second round of the French presidential race looks like a rout. After all, Macron garnered 66 percent support to Le Pen's 34 percent.[61] However, an examination of the whole race suggests that the foundations for the win may be more precarious than they seem at first glance. In the first round of the race that featured Macron, Le Pen, Fillon and Mélenchon, the spread between first place and fourth place was less than 4.5 percent, or fewer than one in 20 voters.

The results suggest that if one of 20 French voters (five percent) had drifted away from Macron, any conceivable second round match up could have occurred. Far-right Le Pen might have faced off against far-left Mélenchon. Centre-right Fillon might have had a show-

Figure 19
2017 French Presidential Election Results - Rounds 1 and 2
(Source: Ministry of the Interior, Republic of France)

Top Four Presidential Candidates	First round		Second round	
	Number votes	% of people who voted for candidate	Number of votes	% of people who voted for candidate
Emmanuel Macron (En Marche!)	8,656,346	24.01	20,753,798	66.10
Marine Le Pen (National Front)	7,678,491	21.30	10,644,118	33.90
François Fillon (Les Républicain)	7,212,995	20.01		
Jean-Luc Mélenchon (la France Insoumise)	7,059,951	19.58		

Source: Ministry of the Interior, Republic of France, http://elections.interieur.gouv.fr/presidentielle-2017/FE.html

61 Résultats de l'élection présidentielle 2017. (n.d.). Ministry of the Interior. Republic of France. Retrieved July 6, 2017, from https://www.interieur.gouv.fr/Elections/Les-resultats/Presidentielles/elecresult__presidentielle-2017/(path)/presidentielle-2017/FE.html.

down against far-right Le Pen. The key point is the fragility of the results, and how very marginal swings could have reshaped the second-round race. Likewise, the candidates (Le Pen and Mélenchon) who appealed to groups that felt marginalized, registered record levels of support. Le Pen, although not successful in the second round, was able to hit a level of support that was a historic high for the far-right with more than 10 million voters supporting her candidacy. She effectively doubled her father's showing as the National Front candidate in the 2002 French presidential election.

Macron's victory was made doubly sweet with a strong win in the parliamentary elections. The presidential majority in the National Assembly, which is comprised of

Figure 20
The hollowing out of the Socialist Party in France
(Source: Ministry of the Interior, Republic of France)

	2012 Election		2017 Election	
	Seats won	%	Seats won	%
Union for a Popular Movement (UMP)	194	37.95%	-	-
New Centre (NC)	12	2.47%	-	-
Miscellaneous Right (DVD)	15	1.81%	6	1.68%
Movement for France (MPF)	-	-	-	-
Socialist Party (PS)	280	40.91%	30	5.68%
French Communist Party (PCF)	-	-	10	1.20%
Miscellaneous Left (DVG)	22	3.08%	12	1.45%
Radical Party of the Left (RDG)	12	2.34%	3	0.36%
The Greens (VEC)	17	3.60%	-	-
Democratic Movement (MoDem)	2	0.49%	42	6.06%
Miscellaneous (DIV)	-	-	3	0.55%
Regionalists and separatists (REG)	2	0.59%	5	0.76%
National Front (FN)	2	3.66%	8	8.75%
Far-left (EXG)	-	-	-	-
Ecologists (ECO)	-	-	1	0.13%
Far-right (EXD)	1	0.13%	1	0.10%
Left Front (FG)	10	1.08%	-	-
Radical Party (PRV)	6	1.35%	-	-
Centrist Alliance (ALLI)	2	0.53%	-	-
La France Insoumise (FI)	-	-	17	4.86%
La République En Marche (REM)	-	-	308	43.06%
The Republicans (LR)	-	-	112	22.23%
Union of Democrats and Independents (UDI)	-	-	18	3.04%
Debout la France (DLF)	-	-	1	0.10%

1 French Legislative Election 2007. Retrieved November 8th, 2017, from

2 French Legislative Election 2012. Retrieved November 8th, 2017, from https://www.interieur.gouv.fr/Elections/Les-resultats/Legislatives/elecresult__LG2012/(path)/LG2012/FE.html

3 French Legislative Election 2017. Retrieved November 8th, 2017, from https://www.interieur.gouv.fr/Elections/Les-resultats/Legislatives/elecresult__legislatives-2017/(path)/legislatives-2017/FE.html

La République En Marche![62] and the Democratic Movement has 350 of the 577 seats: the strongest majority since 1993. In 2017, his former governing Socialist Party dropped from 280 to a mere 30 seats. Of note, in 2017 the Socialist Party saw a corresponding drop in popular support from 41 to 6 percent (see Figure 20). Not only has Macron smashed the party system but he has decimated his former party, the Socialists, in the National Assembly, supplanting them with his six-month-old movement, En Marche!

Even with his strong victory in the French National Assembly election, the results should not be seen as a major setback for the parties on the more extreme parts of the political spectrum. Both Mélenchon and Le Pen for the first time won seats in the French lower house of Parliament and have vowed to continue their fight against Macron. The results of both the presidential and National Assembly elections give Macron a strong mandate to govern France. However, setting aside the election results, fundamental economic challenges still exist.

Jobs, jobs, jobs

During his victory speech, Macron noted, 'I know the divisions in our nation'[63]. The voter rage on the far right and the far left were a result of a number of factors – unemployment rates key among them. Macron's top promises included a focus on fighting unemployment. With youth unemployment near one in four people under 25

62 Following his win, Macron rebranded his party to La République En Marche!
63 Macron wins French presidency, to sighs of relief in Europe. (2017, May 8). Reuters. Retrieved July 6, 2017, from http://ca.reuters.com/article/topNews/idCAKBN183003-OCATP.

in France and the general unemployment rate far higher than in neighbouring Germany, the challenge for Macron will be to create a program of renewal which deals with the margins and those who are economically marginalized. A complication for the French president is the proximity and default comparability to Germany.

France and Germany have a shared history on continental Europe and are among the leading nations in the European Union. They are both major advanced industrial democracies, and share a border. For citizens in both countries, they are natural comparator nations in terms of the economy. The economic data suggests that there are underlying factors in France which can contribute to the success of the extreme right and left, and first among those are unemployment rates. A December 2016 report by Eurostat[64] illustrates a very stark difference in the employment rates in Germany and France.

Figure 21
Unemployment rates Germany and France
(Source: Eurostat, Europa)

	Germany jan-17	France jan-17	Difference
National Unemployment	3.80%	10.00%	2.6 times
Youth under 25	6.50%	23.60%	3.6 times
Male	4.30%	10.10%	2.3 times
Female	3.30%	9.90%	3.0 times

Source: Eurostat produces harmonized unemployment rates for individual EU member states, the euro area and the EU. These unemployment rates are based on the definition recommended by the International Labour Organization (ILO). The measurement is based on a harmonized source, the European Union Labour Force Survey (LFS).

64 Eurostat Press Office. (2017, January 31). Euro area unemployment at 9.6%. Retrieved July 6, 2017, from http://ec.europa.eu/eurostat/documents/2995521/7844069/3-31012017-CP-EN.pdf/f7a98d76-13bc-4586-9e25-9e206e9b6f02.

Although the French unemployment rate is comparable to the Euro Area (EA19) average, it is 2.6 times higher than Germany's. Although Germany outpaces France on items such as exports per capita (Germany's is double that of France), France has a higher birthrate (51 percent more than Germany) and proportion of its population under 14 years of age (43 percent more than Germany).[65] The result is significant economic pressure on the French Republic – much more so comparatively than the Federal Republic of Germany. The key takeaway is that in terms of economic motivations for voter anger, France is comparatively more susceptible than Germany and will continue to be susceptible in the near future. To compound this, the very pro-EU Macron will have to defend his view that the Europe project has been good for France – even in the face of data that suggests that on the jobs front, Germany has benefitted far more. With about one in four young people unemployed, it is uncertain how long the optimism coming out of Macron's big win will last. Certainly, part of his appeal was that he was not Le Pen and not Mélenchon – Macron represented a middle choice. However, in the future, Macron will more likely be judged by his performance as president, not on his comparability to choices which now are set aside until the next election cycle.

65 France and Germany Compared. (n.d.). Retrieved July 6, 2017, from http://www.nationmaster.com/country-info/compare/France/Germany.

So, what can we learn from the French election?

The French election brings into focus a number of nuances when it comes to understanding the rage of voters. In this case, voters resoundingly rejected the established political parties and their leaders, turning to a brand new movement. The Socialist Party, one of the traditional governing parties of France, was decimated in the National Assembly. The ideological margins on the right and the left made historic gains. Although Macron did very well in the second round of the presidential election, the results of the first round should give him pause. If as few as one in 20 voters hadn't voted for Macron, it would have led to an alternative second round run-off and likely different election outcome. This speaks to the fragility of election outcomes and the influence that the margins and the marginalized can have. For Macron it probably explains why, having won major presidential and National Assembly victories, he repeatedly reminds the French nation how divided it is and how hard he is prepared to work to keep France away from the extremes. It also explains how the maverick Rothschild's banker became an agent of change, smashing the French party establishment in the process.

91
92
51
50
49

CANADA
NORTH
AMERICA
U.S.A.
LOS ANGELES
BAJA CALIFORNIA
PACIFIC
HOUSTON
CUBA
VENEZUELA
COLOMBIA

CHAPTER 6
Are Polls Really for the Dogs? How to Read Them Like a Pro

Canada's 13th prime minister, Conservative John Diefenbaker, dismissed polls with a pun, suggesting that dogs knew what to do with them.[66] There have, on occasion, been failures in the ability of public opinion research to accurately capture public opinion. George Gallup, the father of modern public opinion polling, was not himself immune. In the 1948 US presidential election, Gallup predicted Dewey would defeat Truman. In the 1957 Canadian federal election, Gallup predicted that John Diefenbaker had little chance of defeating the Liberals. Gallup got both elections wrong. The reality, however, is that the vast majority of scientifically conducted public opinion polls by reputable firms, using the same tried and true methodologies used in areas such as health, transportation and economic research, accurately capture opinion at the time the survey is conducted. Like air travel, the

66 John George Diefenbaker Quote. (n.d.). Retrieved July 6, 2017, from http://www.quotes.net/quote/63936. Diefenbaker's exact quote was 'I've always been fond of dogs, and they are the one animal that knows the proper treatment to give to poles.'

crashes tragically and spectacularly catch the attention of the public, but air travel remains a very safe way to get from point A to point B.[67] Getting a survey right, like delivering a passenger safely to destination, is not news.

The night of the 2016 US presidential election, at first blush, looked like a crash for the US polling industry. The media, politicians and people on social media were alit over the apparent inability of the pollsters to predict a Trump victory. It was perceived as a failure of polling and many questioned the reliability of public opinion research to capture voter preferences. The national polling suggested Clinton had an advantage in the national popular vote. Nevertheless, Trump won the election and became president. In the end, the poll results and the election results didn't actually turn out to be contradictory. On election night, some analysts claimed that Trump supporters lied to pollsters or were reluctant to tell the truth. The accuracy of the national vote predictions effectively dismisses those claims. Clinton did in fact win the election in terms of the popular vote, but lost the Electoral College vote because of the inefficient distribution of her support. Once all mail-in absentee ballots were counted, the polls were generally proven correct in reflecting the mood of the whole nation, but there was a problem in converting the polling into the Electoral College outcome (see Figure 1). Clinton had a two-percent (or about a three-million-vote) advantage

67 IATA. (2016, February 15). IATA Releases 2015 Safety Performance - No fatal jet hull losses. Retrieved July 6, 2017, from http://www.iata.org/pressroom/pr/Pages/2016-02-15-01.aspx. According to the International Air Transportation Association, the global jet accident rate in 2015 was 0.32 or the equivalent of one major accident for every 3.1 million flights.

over Trump in the national tally for president but Trump won the Electoral College by 14 percentage points.

This disconnect between accurately capturing voter sentiment and converting that sentiment into election outcomes is a key risk in the use of public opinion polling to predict electoral outcomes. It is one thing to predict a level of support and another to predict how that converts into a body like the Electoral College, or the number of seats in a parliamentary democracy in a first past the post system, where popular support never aligns with seat counts. In most parliamentary elections in the UK, majorities in the House of Commons are won without a majority of popular support because of the workings of a winner-take-all system.[68] This disconnect between voting estimates and democratic outcomes, along with declining response rates, pressure on media organizations to be the first to predict outcomes, and changes in polling technology and methodology, are changing the terrain for the research industry.

How about those 'good ol' days' for the polling industry?

From the nascent launch of the polling industry to its maturity, factors such as sample coverage, predictive dialing and rigorous quality control were adopted by many of the key players in the research industry to improve ac-

68 In a first past the post parliamentary system, the winner at the riding level is the candidate with the greatest number of votes. For example, in a three-way race, if three candidates received 34%, 33% and 33% of the vote respectively, the candidate with 34% would win the local riding election and secure the seat. In an extreme example, in a legislature with 100 seats where one party won all the local elections with 34% support with the example cited, it would win all the seats in the legislature 100% but have only 34% nationally.

curacy. Prior to the advent of the Internet, when telephone surveys were the industry standard, it was difficult to enter the industry and there were few players. The cost of entry included building, managing and keeping busy large call centers with live agents who dialed citizens to ask them their opinions. In most democracies, there were handfuls, not multitudes, of stable polling companies that primarily conducted consumer and public policy research and periodically engaged in election research for news organizations as a side line of business.

Mis-calls during elections were in large part a result of the inadequacies of sample coverage where not all the eligible voters had a chance to be randomly selected as part of the national survey. Reliance on samples with listed numbers meant that households with unlisted numbers were not part of the random selection. During the 1960s, when access to computers and current telephone lists were scarce, the lists available to researchers did not have full coverage and were always a year old with the reliance on the printed telephone book. The advent of the Mitofsky-Waksberg sampling method in the 1960s revolutionized the research industry. Warren Mitofsky and Joseph Waksberg pioneered a random digit dialing (RDD) sampling method which is still in use today. This method generates samples based on all potential numbers in a telephone exchange, thus ensuring that listed, unlisted and new telephone numbers all have a chance to be randomly selected in the sample. Esoteric to some, it was a revolution for the survey industry which advanced the reliability of polling and is still used for both land and cell line samples.

Another key element of the good ol' days for the survey industry had to do with response rates. A response rate is the proportion of responses to a survey based on the number of valid phone numbers[69] in the original RDD sample. It was not unusual to have response rates of 25 percent for a live telephone survey. The result was an increasing level of confidence in the data and a cost structure which controlled research budgets. The tolerance for respondents to do longer surveys was also much higher. Fast forward to the present and response rates for telephone interviews of the general populace can be as low as five to ten percent and tolerance for long survey interviews among respondents has dropped. This has implications for the cost to do quality research since it takes more effort to reach the same number of respondents and at the same time less content is collected in the shorter interview. For some, low response rates are a signal that a survey is not reliable.

The evidence suggests that surveys can produce reliable results despite low response rates, so long as they are random samples that include both cell and land line samples that are weighted to match the demographic profile of the target population. In an independent study, the Pew Research Center for the People and the Press conducted parallel low (9%) and higher (22%) response rate studies. The conclusion by Pew, when examining 40 variables between the two studies in 2012, was that the high effort, higher response rate survey had little impact on the

69 Invalid numbers would include, for example, telephone or cell numbers that were not in service or fax numbers. These would be excluded from the calculation for a survey response rate.

quality of the results.[70] This study was repeated in 2017 and the independent research from Pew suggests that low and high response rate telephone studies still conform to each other in terms of results.[71] One item that does appear in the research in terms of non-response is that survey participants in general tend to be more engaged in civic activities compared to non-responders. This non-response bias favours the reliability of survey research for election campaigns because there is likely a relationship between participating in public opinion research and voting. If a citizen is not engaged civically and does not vote, they are probably less likely to participate in a survey. The fact that high quality RDD sample surveys that include both land- and cell-line samples weighted to the population can not only be consistently but strikingly accurate in capturing intentions was witnessed in the 2006 Canadian federal election. In 2006, the survey conducted in the close of the campaign by Nanos Research was an accurate snapshot of the outcome.

Figure 22
Canadian Federal Election Comparison 2006
(Source: Nanos Research)

2006 Federal Election	Nanos Election Poll (January 20th to 22, 2006)	Election results (January 23, 2006)	Variance
Conservative	36.4%	36.3%	0.1
Liberal	30.1%	30.2%	0.1
NDP	17.4%	17.5%	0.1
Bloc	10.6%	10.5%	0.1
Green	5.6%	4.5%	1.1

Source: CPAC/Nanos Nightly Tracking, national random telephone RDD survey, four week rolling average of 1,051 Canadians, accurate ±3.0 percentage points, 19 times out of 20.

70 Gewurz, D. (2012, May 15). Assessing the Representativeness of Public Opinion Surveys. PEW. Retrieved July 6, 2017, from http://www.people-press.org/2012/05/15/assessing-the-representativeness-of-public-opinion-surveys/.

71 Keeter, S., Hatley, N., Kennedy, C., & Lau, A. (2017, May 15). What Low Response Rates Mean for Telephone Surveys. PEW. Retrieved July 6, 2017, from http://www.pewresearch.org/2017/05/15/what-low-response-rates-mean-for-telephone-surveys/.

The reliability of the Nanos Research was due to a combination of a number of factors including the quality of the sample, the clarity of the questions, the quality of the fieldwork team and also the proximity of the fieldwork to election day. One false comparison by many observers is to hold a survey conducted four, five or more days before the election as predictive of the election. If a survey is intended to capture the sentiment on election day, it needs to be conducted either on election day or on the day before. The reason this is the case is that many voters are like Christmas shoppers. Some purchase gifts far in advance of Christmas, others purchase during the Christmas sale season, others the last week before Christmas and some on Christmas Eve. Voting behaviour is no different. Loyal partisans know who they will vote for even before the election, others wait to make a judgement during the election, others wait for the last week and some are last minute deciders. In this world, the proximity of the fieldwork to the actual vote is of critical importance to the accuracy of the research.

Proximity itself, however, is no guarantee of reliability. A look at the polling in the 2017 British general election suggests a mixed bag of performance for the pollsters in Great Britain. At one end of the spectrum were YouGov and Survation, both of which pointed to a hung parliament with no majority for any party, while the other pollsters showed between a six- and 12-point Conservative advantage and a majority win. The key differentiator for the pollsters who were incorrect were post field adjustments, which amplified the projection in favour of the Conservatives. In their attempt to be more accurate, they adjusted their numbers. This is a standard practice for a number of public opinion research firms, and consistently provides mixed results as pollsters try to model who will vote. The adjustment models can be subjective in nature, building on assumptions that may not bear themselves out. In an ideal world, the return sample generally mirrors the population surveyed, requires minimal weighting and reflects the views of those interviewed. For example, the research conducted by Nanos does not model for the anticipated profile of voters on Election Day but relies on probability sampling to naturally capture opinion.

In contrast to the mixed results in the 2017 UK election, the pollsters in France performed quite well in the first round of the presidential election. In the second round of the election, the overall estimations were correct in terms of the outcome, but Emmanuel Macron's vote was marginally underestimated. Considering the last poll was conducted two days before the vote and not the day before, the polling results did well in capturing opinion. For example, Ipsos estimated the support for Macron on May 5 at 63 percent, and his final level of support was 66 percent. With a vote on May 7, 2017, there was still an extra day. To attain the highest level of precision, one needs to survey as close to voting day as possible.

One significant change to polling from the past is the emergence of new research technologies. Among the most revolutionary has been the advent and proliferation of online surveys. Online surveys have generally reduced the cost of research and added a level of content capability that is very compelling. Online surveys are a cost-effective platform to test creative concepts and explore complex topics. After all, if one is testing a logo for a company, one can't quite show the logo through a telephone interview. Online, one can display and have respondents interact with visual content. Similarly, interactive voice response surveys, where automated voices prompt respondents over the phone to press '1' for a particular answer and press '2' for another particular answer, represent a cost effective and very fast means of conducting research.

The diversity of methodologies, including telephone with live agents, online and interactive voice response (IVR), means that in some instances work conducted over the same period by different methodologies can yield the same or different results. Likewise, some online surveys are panel surveys (where people voluntarily join to share their opinion) and others are random online surveys which look to have a random component. For example, a potential respondent can be recruited with live agents through a land and cell line sample and asked to do an online survey. This diversity of method is compounded by differences in the wording and the order of questions which can have a significant influence on the results of individual surveys. When the industry was dominated by few pollsters who exclusively used random telephone surveys with live agents, outlier results were exactly that – exceptions that periodically occurred. Fast forward to a world with a diversity of methodologies and there is an increasing likelihood of a lack of consensus on the research. For example, the *LA Times*' online methodology was more likely to consistently have Trump in the lead nationally, while other pollsters had a closer race or Clinton in the lead. This contrast had a number of implications. First, it casts a shadow on the research industry, since it had competing projections. Second, it allows voters or campaigns to 'pick their poll', where supporters of a campaign will cite the poll favourable to them and dismiss the poll which is unfavourable. Third, the emergence of the aggregators who seek to smooth over the polling variations to satisfy the media thirst for predictions further exacerbated negative views of polling research.

What the Vegas bookie and the polling aggregator have in common

It's all about the odds – that is, the probability of one outcome over another. Among the more famous aggregators is Nate Silver of FiveThirtyEight.com. Silver is a one stop shop for political junkies. On his site, he aggregates and analyzes polls from a diversity of sources and generates the probability of likely outcomes. In one respect, the emergence and influence of Nate Silver was a response to the increasing diversity and number of polls in the public domain. The aggregators were there to hedge the risk for the media of relying on an outlier survey. After all, more surveys in the aggregation model made for a better prediction, right? Actually, this is not always the case.

Aggregators such as Nate Silver are hostage to the quality of the inputs they use in their model. They are not pollsters themselves, since the inputs are those of other organizations. They are aggregators that triage, compile and analyze data from a series of external inputs and put them in a model. The risk for the aggregator is that if one or more of the inputs are outliers or of low-quality, it puts their model at risk compared to a high-quality survey. A high-quality reliable survey will always beat the aggregator in the same way that the aggregator will always beat a low-quality survey. Another challenge is the way that outsiders misunderstand the probability of outcomes. For example, FiveThirtyEight.com estimated that Hillary Clinton had a 71.4 percent chance of victory while Trump had a 28.6 percent chance of winning the presidency.[72] This did not mean that Clinton would win the presidency, but was taken to by many. Likewise, the model still showed there was a chance of Trump winning. On election day, Democrat political junkies who visited FiveThirtyEight.com likely thought that although it was a close election, Clinton would prevail. This was a false comfort because not only did Silver have to rely on a diversity of national polling data but also a diversity of the state level data needed to help understand the dynamic of the Electoral College. Silver, like the pollsters,

72 Silver, N. (2016, November 08). 2016 Election Forecast. Retrieved July 6, 2017, from https://projects.fivethirtyeight.com/2016-election-forecast/.

was accurate in estimating the outcome of the popular vote. However, the model fell short in bridging popular sentiment with the Electoral College. In that respect, the Las Vegas bookie and the aggregators have one thing in common. They are hostage to the inputs to create odds and when they lose, they can lose big.

Among the more interesting additions to public opinion forecasting has been research that uses search-term or social media analysis to predict election outcomes. This is a new field that merits attention, but with caution. For example, in 2008 Google sought to estimate the potential breakout of the flu by using an algorithm applied to millions of search terms input by Internet users. On the surface, this made sense. Google could harness millions of data inputs and map a potential outbreak. An examination by researchers at Northwestern University suggests that the Google algorithm consistently overestimates flu prevalence over time. The outcome is big headlines that do not necessarily match up with reality. As the authors of the study put it, it's 'big data hubris'[73]. Similar emerging work has been done in the area of measuring social media sentiment and claiming that social media sentiment accurately captured a Trump victory. However, if this is the case, then the social media sentiment did not accurately capture real voter sentiment as indicated by the popular vote support for Clinton and does not reflect the reality that a very small swing of vot-

73 Lazer, D., Kennedy, R., King, G., & Vespignani, A. (2014, March 14). The Parable of Google Flu: Traps in Big Data Analysis. Science Magazine. Retrieved July 6, 2017, from http://gking.harvard.edu/files/gking/files/0314policyforumff.pdf.

ers made Trump president. One should be careful in directly conflating social media sentiment with voter intentions. This becomes even riskier when one factors in the increasing number of political bots on social media that automatically retweet and like posts from various candidates, which can skew social media activity. Even with this, measuring social media sentiment in terms of who is winning the propaganda war is likely a more fruitful research line of inquiry, because citizens engaged in social media are influenced by the social media ecosystem.

Perhaps the key conclusion from a look at data intent on capturing sentiment and projecting outcomes is 'caveat emptor' or 'buyer beware'. A diversity of survey methodologies exists and these are less comparable than in the past. More data does not mean better data – it only means more data. The aggregators who look to hedge on the diversity of polling data are hostage to the quality of their inputs. People project outcomes on the data (like the Electoral College votes or seat projections in a parliamentary democracy) which are a statistical stretch prone to even greater estimation variability. The very competitive media market, with a business model under pressure, is hard pressed to fund quality research and prefers clear and straightforward headlines, as opposed to nuanced interpretations on the chance of one electoral outcome over another.

In a world of polarized political parties, where very small swings have a disproportionate impact on outcomes, reliable public opinion research will be in demand. Looking at the track record of a research organization and the proximity of the fieldwork to election day will become increasingly important as the social media space is gamed by campaigns and other actors seeking to influence voters. In the same way that politicians should understand the real fragility of a campaign win as a snapshot of support on election day only, citizens and those who look at public opinion polling will need to better contextualize the polling data and the complex shades of grey that make up the electorate.

STILL WE RISE
HEAR OUR VOICE
WE DESERVE BETTER
STOP THE GASLIGHTING SUPPORT THE PRESS
LIBERTY and JUSTICE for ALL
KEEP YOUR
Wahine POWER
WOMEN'S MARCH
TRUMP LIKES
ICKELBACK
LESS FOLLY MORE DOLLY
CONGRESS
ANTI
HEALTH CARE
equality
LGBTQIA+ EQUALITY
RESPECT WOMEN OF COLOR
LGBTQIA+ EQUALITY

TOP

★ 10 ★

CHAPTER 7
The Age of Voter Rage Top Ten: What Did We Learn?

At the heart of voter rage is emotion. Like many things, the drivers of emotion are as diverse as the voters within each country. It can be driven by economic factors like losing a home, being paid less, or having difficulty keeping up with expenses. It can extend to concern about immigrants and the threat to personal safety or jobs security. It can also be driven by the fear of the extremes, as illustrated by the French election – fear countering the rage of the margins. This book sought to explore how voter behaviour has manifested in different countries. The value of a cross-country comparison is to unpack commonalities beyond the idiosyncrasies of individual nations. Its purpose is to challenge people to consider whether the anger in other countries is a contagion that might spread to their home nation. The following observations help advance a better understanding of what is happening. Although some may assert the emergence of populism as an ideology, it has thin ideological consistency across nations. Voter rage is as diverse and multifaceted as the countries within which it manifests. It leans neither to the right nor left, is identifiably populist in style but should by no means be confused with any kind of belief system or political ideology. There are, however, commonalities in the experiences across a number of democracies.

This is an anti-establishment movement

The political players trying to tap into the rage of voters share the strategy of identifying and criticizing the establishment. While anti-establishment populism is not new (presidential candidate Ross Perot in the US, the Reform Party in Canada, far-right parties in Europe), what is new is the success that politicians are now having tapping into this anger. Trump in the US attacked the political establishment in Washington, the establishment within his own Republican party, Wall Street, and the global trade order. Farage and the Brexiteers in the UK referendum vote targeted the establishment of the European Union and London financial elites. Corbyn in the 2017 UK election set his sights on attacking the class establishment, and Macron in France mobilized voters against the traditional party establishment. In Canada, the positive and progressive Justin Trudeau reshaped his image to one more aligned with an anti-establishment style, taking on a boxing match and targeting the richest one percent for tax hikes, to advance a liberal narrative asserting that the incumbent conservative government of a decade had let average Canadians down and had the wrong priorities.

This anti-establishment ethos quickly expands into attacks on media establishments with claims of bias and is dismissive of any criticism, fact or argument counter to the anti-establishment message being advanced. It is populist in the sense that it seeks to advocate and fight for the common person against the elites but is, as coined by the University of Georgia's Cas Mudde, a 'thin ideology'[74] – simplistic. It is about the common person, 'us', versus the elite 'them'. Beyond the basic reduction to a black and white world, the evidence presented is anecdotal and solutions proposed are very contextual. A new immigrant murders a citizen – it is a failure of the establishment to protect citizens. A factory is closed – the establishment's pursuit of trade deals results in lost jobs at home. In this view, elites make bad decisions and are hostage to big money and lobbyists, while the people suffer. Very small swings in voters have a major impact on outcomes.

A review of the data in the US election, Brexit referendum and Canadian election suggests that very small swings in voters significantly shape democratic outcomes. In that sense, one should not confuse 'populist movements' pitting the common citizen against elites with 'popular movements' which represent the vast majority of citizens in a democracy. Here is the numerical cheat sheet.

74 What is populism? (2016, December 19). The Economist. Retrieved July 6, 2017, from http://www.economist.com/blogs/economist-explains/2016/12/economist-explains-18.

Figure 23
Tyranny of Small Swings at a Glance

	Swing Margin*	Total Ballots Cast	Swing Percentage of Total Ballots Cast	**Tyranny of the Small Swing**	Alternative Outcome
French Presidential Election Round 1 (2017)	1,956,395	36,054,394	5.43%	**1 in 20 voters**	If 1 in 20 drifted away from Macron he may not have made it to the second round.
UK General Election (2017)	379,500	32,142,000	1.18%	**1 in 100 voters**	Dead heat in aggregate votes between Labour and Conservatives
US Presidential Election (2016)	40,000	137,000,000	0.03%	**1 in 3,333 voters**	From a Trump win in Electoral College to a Clinton win
UK Referendum (2016)	650,000	33,500,000	1.94%	**1 in 50 voters**	From a Leave to a Remain Victory
Canadian Federal Election (2015)	880,000	17,592,000	5.00%	**1 in 20 voters**	From a Liberal majority to a minority government

* number of changed votes that would have reshaped outcomes.

Democracy is very much about who shows up to vote. When voter turnout is average or below average, small, highly motivated sub-segments of the electorate, activated by populist-style politicians, can disproportionately shape the types of governments elected. The mandates of governments are much more fragile than the definitive results of a vote suggest. In many cases, the mere shift in preferences of 1 in 20 voters is enough to unseat a government or to weaken a majority government in the elected legislature to minority status. A one in 20 shift in the political mood, that is five percent, could be a net 10-point swing from one party to another. Winners tend to forget the strength of victory and often confuse stability in the legislature for four years with stability in the electorate. Most times there is a disconnect. An election is a snapshot in time – specifically and only on election day. Sentiment and preferences change the day after the election, subject to the new government's track record and how it responds to events.

What is critical is that in a world where democratic outcomes are shaped by very small swings in opinion, where the political margins are growing, the marginalized, when they show up to vote, can have a significant impact on how a country will be governed and will make or break politicians and political parties.

Voter rage is not only a right-wing phenomenon

These populist anger movements, which can be thin on ideology, are about citizens searching for politicians who can be instruments of punishment for the establishment. In some cases, these can be right-wing politicians, in other cases progressive or left-wing politicians. Politicians like Donald Trump in the US, Nigel Farage in the UK and Marine Le Pen in France are decidedly more right-wing. However, Corbyn and Macron and Trudeau are decidedly progressive. Justin Trudeau in Canada framed himself as anti-establishment in style, a different kind of politician compared to Conservative Prime Minister Stephen Harper, and tapped into the middle class's anxiety about the future and anger at the government to unseat the incumbent government with a positive progressive message. Macron in France abandoned his Socialist Party and with his win in the presidential and National Assembly elections reshaped the party system in France. His non-establishment En Marche! movement and maverick outsider style appealed to those concerned about the rise of extremism on both the right and the left. These changes can manifest themselves through right, left and centrist movements. The primary frame of those angry voters is quite simply: 'Who do I vote for to send a message and punish the elite establishment?'

This class war is between the educated and the less educated

An analysis of the data suggests that the appeal and success of anti-establishment politicians is greater when looking at educational attainment instead of income. Income and education do relate to each other but the divisions are much starker when you look at them through an education lens. Voters in the UK and the US had a greater tendency to align with anti-establishment populist choices if they did not have a university or equivalent education. They can vote for anti-establishment options if they do have high incomes but the strongest relationship is based on schooling and not income. Research in the last presidential election in the US and also the Brexit vote in the UK suggests that there was a relationship between embracing anti-establishment options and a lower educational attainment. The same was very true in the Brexit vote where the Leave forces did well in areas where the incidence of higher educational attainment voters was lower than average.

The anti-establishment, anti-elite, anti-intellectual mantra of politicians looking to promote voter anger is more likely to have traction among voters who have a lower educational attainment. The important emerging division to monitor is education. This frame also likely explains how fuzzy truth and unreliable political promises have permeated this new environment. In the United States presidential election, high educational attainment voters took Donald Trump at his word to build a wall between the US and Mexico and to tear up the North American Free Trade Agreement, and were skeptical knowing that delivering on those promises was much more complex than presented by Trump. For Americans with a lower education attainment, those same promises were symbolic, not only of their concerns but also of Trump's political resolve to fight for the common citizen. This education division also better explains the two solitudes among voters – neither side can empathize with or understand the rationalizations of the other.

Economic factors are the trigger but differ across nations

Although one cannot point to a single economic indicator – such as real wages or the cost of living – as the trigger to activate angry voters, there is a common theme. Triggers are related to the economy either directly or indirectly. Economic factors are symbols for populists to leverage. In the United States, jobs lost to trade or homes lost in the great recession are powerful symbols to activate angry voters. In the United Kingdom, the perceived export of money to the EU (and the promise to repatriate tax money for the National Health Service), a decline in real wages and a rising cost of living for average citizens were central elements of the frame voters used to judge the decision on Great Britain's future relationship with the European Union. In Canada, the sense of declinism – that is, the view that the standard of living would be worse for future generations of Canadians – coupled with a flat economy was the opportunity for the opposition Liberals led by Trudeau to engage Canadians, advance a middle-class agenda taxing the top one percent of income earners and unseat the Conservative incumbent government. The French mindset is likely one of comparable decline vis-à-vis the Germans. Both France and Germany are members of the EU, but French unemployment is significantly higher than Germany's. Thus, a neighbour's envy can fuel voter sentiment.

Anger politics is contagious between nations

It's the copycat syndrome. The US presidential election proved a number of things, including that populist-style politics that leverage social media can break the influence of big money on elections. Likewise, massive formal political machinery is not as important to deliver angry voters who get themselves to the ballot booth without the help of the party. Twenty-four hour campaigning through personal appearance by day and social media in the sleeping hours can drive media coverage and attract the attention of voters. For aspiring politicians in any country looking to break in as outsiders, these are very practical and appealing tips to cut through the democratic clutter in one's home country. The success of Donald Trump in the United States and the Brexit forces in Great Britain make them models, controversial for some, to be emulated by other politicians. What works in one country gets tried in another.

One implication of concern is that if a leading politician makes racist remarks, it gives social license to citizens to advance racist views and to behave as racists. Similarly, if a leading politician condones violence, it gives political license to followers to behave violently. Followers take their cues from those they follow. This is the contagion between politicians in different countries. Another dimension of the contagion is between nations, where anger is directed at neighbour countries and creates an 'us and them' mentality between nations. Donald Trump focused on the loss of jobs and on illegal immigrants and what he described as 'bad hombres' from Mexico as key problems he would fix as president. Marine Le Pen declared that if she led France, she would fight 'savage globalization' and not 'submit' to Germany's Angela Merkel and the European Union elite. The Eurosceptic Leave forces in Great Britain fought what they believed was a corrupt EU.

The observation is that populist style politics promote copy cat politicians in other countries. Also, parties are influenced by the successes and tribulations of other ideologically similar movements in other countries. Pasokification, where a governing socialist party in Greece went from government to being decimated by voters in favour of a more extreme left-wing option, was a wake-up call for many socialist organizers. Corbyn in the UK veered his party farther left. The former Socialist Party in France was abandoned by centrist Macron and far-leftist Mélenchon, both of whom created new movements which tapped into voter rage against the party establishments.

Anger movements trigger counter-anger mobilization

The victory of an anger movement, in effect, becomes the wake-up call for counter-mobilization. In the United States, the enormity of the Women's March the day after Donald Trump's inauguration was the clarion call for the anti-Trump forces to mobilize and organize. The open divisions within the US populace during the election extended past the campaign: Trump registered the lowest approval rating of an incoming president in the modern era as Americans failed to rally behind their new president. In Great Britain, after the Brexit victory, individuals crowd-funded a legal case to jail lying politicians. They identified what they considered the big lie, the repatriation of funding for the National Health Service, as the prime example to bring politicians before the courts for punishment.

Voter rage is increasingly becoming a global and quite complex new political ecosystem which has national, bi-national and global implications. A common trait is that the tactics of the anger movement in one nation, xenophobia, racism, anti-globalism, focus on symbolic rather than literal messaging and mistruths, conveys a certain sense of permission for politicians to act the same in other countries for political gain. One should not think of these as uni-directional. The future will involve movements and counter-movements both of the extremes and against the extremes. Although the polarization of the electorate has already been a phenomenon in many democracies, the emerging anger of nations may exacerbate that polarization and convert what is now ballot-box polarization into broader and more open political activism between opposing forces in a democracy. In this environment, one can expect more heated political dialogue on social media and media comments pages, and more formal large and small scale protests by opposing forces.

Social media, not parties, will be increasingly important for political mobilization

The traditional paradigm where formal political parties are the organizing forces for citizens is under siege. Not only are citizens less trustful of all institutions including political parties, but citizens can engage in political dialogue and support causes independent of parties through the platform of social media. Social media is the ready-made platform for anti-establishment political engagement because it is outside of the party system. Movements looking to find followers can do just that very cost-effectively through social media. Donald Trump rightly credited social media in his insurgent campaign to win the

Republican nomination and then the general election for president. Justin Trudeau in Canada has also used social media quite effectively, as did Nigel Farage and Marine Le Pen. In this paradigm, building and engaging personal followers on social media is cost- and time-effective and makes politics more personality driven. The medium has simplified the message and voters are increasingly being drawn into infotainment and making decisions based on image. Trump, Macron, Trudeau – perhaps in the new paradigm boring leaders will have more difficulty getting elected. Building followers and creating entertaining social media experiences allows politicians to amplify messages through re-tweeting and sharing, to direct messages to followers without the use of the mainstream media or traditional advertising. Social media has been a key technological enabler for politicians; this is especially true for politicians that are outsiders or fighting the establishment.

There is a battle waging between symbolism and the facts

The truth is the first casualty of this new age in two respects. First, if a voter is looking to send a message and punish the establishment because they have lost their home, are under-employed or feel threatened by trade, one can argue that their first objective is to realize an objective – in that case, punishment. The objective is not to evaluate the veracity of a claim or promise made by any politician. This is compounded by cynicism as to the truthfulness of any statement made by a politician. Many voters expect politicians' statements won't be completely true or will be distorted to make a point.

The emergence and increasing importance of a 'fact-checking' cottage industry illustrates that enough mistruths are said by politicians to merit both tracking and scoring politicians on their truthfulness. Politicians' lies, compounded with a general declining confidence in the media as unbiased intermediaries of news information and opinions, mean the current environment lacks a common understanding of what can actually be trusted as fact. The emergence of what some partisans euphemistically call 'alternative facts' for transparent public events such as the attendance at Trump's inauguration is part of a broader trend to be fast and loose with the truth. This reminds some of the novel *Nineteen Eighty-Four*, George Orwell's dystopian view of politics driven by the cult of personality and a Ministry of Truth to advance historical revisionism. It surely is no coincidence that along with the emergence of voter rage there has been a rise in book sales for dystopian novels such as Orwell's *Nineteen Eighty-Four* and *The Handmaid's Tale* by Margaret Atwood.

Connecting polling to democratic outcomes will be more difficult

Polling in all the votes examined did a good job at charting the direction of voter sentiment and generally in projecting national voter sentiment. However, converting national sentiment into concrete democratic outcomes, whether it be the connection of polling to Electoral College votes in the US or connecting national sentiment to the number of seats in the House of Commons in Canada, becomes more problematic. This is where the expectations of the media and the public do not match the science of public opinion research. The media and the public want to know who is going to win. Any survey only points to the likelihood of a certain level of support for a particular party or candidate. Likewise, outside of the parties themselves, few media outlets and fewer third parties have the financial resources or interest to fund the major polling needed to predict an election with a level of granularity needed to have confidence in the research.

This is compounded by the situation wherein very small shifts in voter sentiment have a significant influence on the shape of democratic outcomes. Polling needs to be able to identify and track very small swings in sentiment. Controlling for error, whether it be sampling coverage, question design or field quality, is difficult at best. In the absence of greater funding for non-partisan polling in the public domain, expectations need to be adjusted. Although the media and the public can expect a pollster to be accurate within a prescribed statistical variance, caution should be exercised in connecting polling to Electoral College votes or seat projections in a first-past-the-post electoral regime.

In this environment, research organizations must be independent of partisan association. It will not only be critical for research organizations to accurately predict public opinion, but for them to pro-actively focus on being transparent and non-partisan information sources.

```
length,c+
.push(a[c
nction h()
ser_logged
ace(/ +(?=
b = [], c
0 == r(
c = {
} b.1
```

CHAPTER 8
Trolls, Bots and Computational Propaganda: How Democracy is Being Rewired

Trip trap, trip trap. Those are the opening words from the Norwegian fairy tale, written in the 1840s, known as the *Three Billy Goats Gruff*. It is the sound of a billy goat using a bridge to cross a stream. The story chronicles a troll under a bridge who threatens to eat anyone who tries to cross it. The troll gets knocked by the third Billy Goat Gruff into the stream and is swept away. This troll story has a happy ending. When it comes to today's Internet trolls and their impact on democracy, though, one can argue that the story has yet to fully unfold and that the ending in terms of impact on democratic discourse might not be so happy.

Considering the impact of small swings in voter preferences when political options are increasingly representing the margins, social media is the new wilderness that sways political dialogue and vote decisions. In this wild and wicked west, there are no rules and there may or may not be facts. It is unfiltered and can enable, through the guise of anonymity, animosity, hatred and division.

The mythic ugly troll of children's fairy tales has remade itself as the Internet troll: slang for an online disruptor of dialogue. The Internet troll uses inflammatory language to bait and cajole, with a prime interest in disruption. It can be both a noun (the person who engages in that activity) and a verb (the action of 'trolling'). The intersection of Internet trolls, automated bots waging war to influence public opinion, computational propaganda, and the effect of small swings in voters creates one of the more worrisome trends in political discourse.

The world of Internet trolls and bots

'A great compliment' – that was Trump's Twitter response in 2013 to an individual who called him the most superior troll on the whole of Twitter.[75] Even before his presidential run, Trump recognized the Internet trolling sub-culture as a potentially powerful force to harness for political advantage. Like the Internet trolls, he was an outsider, anti-establishment in tone, dismissive of political correctness and in turn dismissed by elites. He was ready to disrupt what he claimed was a rigged and rotten political and economic system in favour of Americans who had lost jobs to globalization. The difference was that he was not anonymous. Trump was to be the vehicle for punishing the establishment while the technological-

75 Trump, D. J. (2013, April 24). Trump Tweet. Retrieved July 6, 2017, from https://twitter.com/realdonaldtrump/status/326970029461614594.

ly savvy troll sub-culture was to be his enabler. Bulletin boards such as 4chan are the anti-establishment ground zero for this decentralized but very influential movement of individuals. Although 4chan itself is an imageboard website initially used to discuss Japanese anime, it has morphed into a home and organization point for the alt-right movement, an amalgam of forces organized against political correctness, grounded in white nationalism. The object is to disrupt order and the establishment, using a combination of Internet memes, sarcasm and mobilization. The arrival of Donald Trump as the outsider Republican nominee for president of the United States created a focus, even purpose, for the alt-right 4chan forces. The combination of anti-establishment fervor with bot and bot-net Internet technology represents a significant new force shaping elections today.

Research at the Oxford Internet Institute by Philip Howard has put a spotlight on the shape, scope and impact of this new force. According to Howard, botnet is a combination of the words 'robot' and 'network' and is a 'collection of programs that communicate across multiple devices to perform a task … such as deploying or replicating messages … or advancing political causes'[76]. According to a 2016 annual study by Incapsula which examined of 16.7 billion visits to 100,000 randomly selected domains, humans (real people) made up 48.2% of Internet traffic while bots comprised the majority (51.8%) of online traffic on the Internet, with the single largest seg-

76 Phil Howard (2015). (n.d.). Bots, Botnets and Political Culture [Prezi]. Retrieved July 6, 2017, from http://www.philhoward.org/.

ment of visits (24.3%) being ones from bots that assumed false identities.[77] This extends into social media platforms such as Twitter and Facebook which are increasingly influencing both voters and the media.

In a media environment characterized by disruption both in terms of business and new models, journalists have increasingly used social media to assess the interest and traction of potential stories. Tweets with high 'like' or 'retweet' counts merit a second look at items which are potentially newsworthy and of interest to consumers of the news. Social media, though, is vulnerable to the same influence of bots as the Internet in general. For example, in 2016, Twitteraudit estimated that of the 22 million followers of the @realDonaldTrump account, more than 16 million were real and six million (or 27%) were fake followers, compared to the @HillaryClinton account, which had 2.8 million (21%) fake followers.[78] Social bots emulate real people with automated tweets in support or opposition of a candidate. This suggests that the popularity, unpopularity or breadth of discourse on a social media interaction should be very closely examined because of the possibility of a false positive which distorts the interactions of real citizens on social media. Social media bot-wars between campaigns to inflate both followers and likes are a hidden, but powerful, reality.

When linked to big data, this creates an environ-

77 Zeifman, I. (2017, January 24). Bot Traffic Report 2016. Retrieved July 6, 2017, from https://www.incapsula.com/blog/bot-traffic-report-2016.html.

78 How many of your followers are real? (n.d.). Retrieved July 6, 2017, from https://www.twitteraudit.com/realdonaldtrump. How many of your followers are real? (n.d.). Retrieved July 6, 2017, from https://www.twitteraudit.com/hillaryclinton.

ment where citizens could be influenced by bots on social media. New research in the area of computational propaganda may be among the most important new lines of academic inquiry intersecting politics, big data and technology. According to Philip Howard from the Oxford Internet Institute, computational propaganda is 'the use of information and communications technologies to manipulate perceptions, affect cognition and influence behaviour … political bots are amongst the latest, and most pervasive, innovations in computational propaganda.'[79] Not only does big data have the ability to deliver bespoke social media messaging on behalf of campaigns, but political bots looking to influence voters are part of the political environment. Those bots can be officially linked to the campaign, or not. Even if they only exert an influence among a minority of voters, a few voters effectively targeted can significantly influence the shape or outcome of elections. As noted before, outcomes are shaped by swings among very small subsets of voters. If a mere one in 20 voters changed their mind because of social media interactions driven by political bots powered by computational propaganda and big data, an election outcome could be substantively influenced. This level of influence has an international dimension as foreign powers, or anyone for that matter, have the capability to influence democratic outcomes or destabilize political dialogue anywhere social media exists.

---

79 Howard, P. (2016, September 20). Computational Propaganda (COMPROP). The Impact of Algorithms and Automation on Public Life [Prezi] Retrieved July 6, 2017, from https://prezi.com/b_vewutjwzut/computational-propaganda/?webgl=0.

A path forward

Although anger is a valid democratic expression, assuming it is non-violent, there are a series of side effects. The top 10 observations cover the issues, which range from the distorting effect of small swings in voter preferences to mistruths in our political dialogue and general dissatisfaction with the system. Disconnectedness with democracy is occurring in many countries across the whole political spectrum. This includes citizens who are concerned about the growth of the 'nanny state' that tells everyone what to think and what to do, through to those who worry about income inequality and how diminished economic mobility creates an underclass of citizens who cannot realize their potential. Likewise, identity politics fuels the concept wherein some citizens feel like strangers in their own land as the diversity in their communities and social norms of the past related to family and faith are being redefined by society and the state.

On the positive side of the ledger, the data suggests that the focus should be citizens who feel politically and economically marginalized, who feel that their vote doesn't count, that the system is failing. They are not a majority but a very important minority starting to be more democratically engaged and enabled by social media to share their views in the public sphere. As non-partisan small groups of voters looking for change and to send a message to the establishment, they are the angry tail wagging the democratic dog.

Voter rage manifests itself differently in each nation subject to the national circumstance and environment. The movement of voters and the forces at play are similar. Small swings are influencing outcomes, the politicians they elect and how they govern. The economically marginalized are turning to both the ideological left and the right, or to outsiders. In this world, traditional establishment parties are either punished by voters (like the Socialist Party in France) or need to remake themselves into anti-establishment movements (as with the Labour Party in the UK).

Some paths forward follow. Some may call them unworkable or unreasonable but they are intended to spur further discussion and are targeted at the different players in our democracy.

Cast light on the bots and the trolls

The potential influence and distorting effects of political bots in social media are a significant challenge to democratic dialogue. For example, according to recent academic research from the Oxford Internet Institute, 'in Michigan, one of the key battleground states, junk news was shared just as widely as professional news in the days leading up to the election.'[80] This points to the potential reach of fake news, which can in some instances become mainstream experience. Setting aside the potential destabilizing influence of foreign players on election outcomes, the increasing use of bots and fake news creates

80 Howard, P. N., Bolsover, G., Kollanyi, B., Bradshaw, S., & Neudert, L. (2017, March 26). Junk News and Bots during the U.S. Election: What Were Michigan Voters Sharing Over Twitter? Retrieved July 6, 2017, from http://comprop.oii.ox.ac.uk/wp-content/uploads/sites/89/2017/03/What-Were-Michigan-Voters-Sharing-Over-Twitter-v2.pdf.

false information experiences and distributes potential mistruths intended to influence voters. The mischaracterization of bots as people distorts that truth and undermines the democratic process.

This is in stark contrast to the Internet troll phenomenon, which is not likely to go away. Although distasteful, it is a valid democratic expression; however, it needs to be contextualized to the proportion of citizens that have those views – not amplified beyond reality. Piercing the anonymous aegis of trolls could help bring some sort of transparency and perhaps ameliorate the bullying political tone. Diversity of opinion is one of the pillars of democracy. Distortion of reality or external interference in the domestic affairs of a nation is not a pillar of democracy. Democracies need to create strategies to encourage interaction between real citizens and to protect voters from manufactured algorithms posing as real citizens.

Win with a tribe but govern for all

The emerging franchise for victory in this new environment is motivate your core voters, mobilize those who hate your enemy and get over-the-top with those who are disconnected with the establishment. The first two parts of the franchise are a traditional winning base; it is the need to appeal to the anti-establishment population to win that can likely disproportionately influence the governing tendencies of electoral winners. Here it is not even the majority of supporters that necessarily influence how a winner governs; it is a minority within the winning franchise.

Governments and politicians of all stripes need to make a tighter connection between decisions and their effects on citizens. In an environment driven by wedge politics intended to activate pockets of voters, more focus needs to be given to groups who feel economically marginalized. Politicians win by mobilizing pockets of voters but, once victorious, ideally govern for the broader public good – the mainstream and the marginalized. Governing policies should be sensitive to this. This is akin to taking a page from the Hippocratic Oath administered to doctors: 'Into whatsoever houses I enter, I will enter to help the sick, and I will abstain from all intentional wrong-doing and harm'. Of course, no policy course is without adverse effects, but the cure should not do more damage than the sickness. In Canada, accepting Syrian refugees was controversial but was framed not only in terms of it being the right thing to do, but also in terms of Canada needing newcomers and the screening process being stringent.

This 'do no harm' lens should apply to both politicians and citizens. For politicians, it should be about focusing on making society better. For citizens, it should be about trying to make elected officials more accountable for their proposals and about minimizing overall harm and maximizing overall good. In this respect, winners need to govern both for their coalition and the marginalized to bring more stability to the political environment.

Fight the mood of declinism

Declinism, or the view that neighbourhoods, the economy, nations and the world are on the decline, is a key challenge. In a workplace, if a team thinks the company is on the decline, is pessimistic, and has an uncertain future, engagement is difficult and the culture of declinism becomes a self-fulfilling prophecy. One could argue that the same holds true for democracy. A democracy gripped by citizen attitudes of declinism fundamentally sees democracy and society failing to create an environment where individuals can realize their potential. Democracies need to provide citizens with the hope that future generations will have at least the same standard of living and perhaps a better standard of living. In the past, the baseline expectation was that our children would have the same or a better standard of living than their parents. Now, many citizens across a number of countries believe that the standard of living will get worse. The primary narrative of the world economy is change, the portability of jobs and the uncertainty of prosperity. In the past, parents could suggest areas of the economy – such as the high tech or manufacturing sectors – that had job opportunities. Now, the one certainty is disruption, automation and uncertainty. This pessimistic narrative of the future is an angry flashpoint for today and tomorrow.

Identify an economic winner

The one fundamental spark for anger and wet blanket on hope is an economy's inability to create prosperity and jobs for citizens. Many industrial economies are shifting from a growth to a low- or no-growth model. This is driven by a new generation – the millennials conditioned for things to be low- or no-cost: Apps, services, and the news. The problem is that free or low-cost items do not yield many jobs. We are not only seeing income inequality among citizens; we are also seeing income inequality among companies. Technology today fuels a winner-take-all paradigm where success is concentrated – Uber, Amazon, Google. If one works for a winner, great. If one works for a loser or a second-tier competitor, one is at risk. The low or slow growth model saps the hope of citizens. Automation and the increasing future application of machine learning will remake the workforce and will continue to be a major economic disruptor. As technology increases productivity and eliminates jobs, citizens may become more xenophobic and anti-immigrant, hostage to a personal economic imperative and counter to their humanitarian nature. On a practical basis, when citizens know where or what the future jobs might be, or which sectors are economic winners, it gives them and their children economic comfort and it helps support a more open and diverse society.

Shake up news organizations

If truthful and quality information is the currency with which voters make informed political decisions, independent-minded and unbiased news organizations are critical to democracy. The blurring of opinion and the news, and the importance of fact-checking, point to the need for news organizations to do more than survive.

As has been written earlier in this book, in a world increasingly influenced by fake news, journalists are the only practical bulwark against falsehoods. The courts are too slow, the citizens lack the power to block a lie and politicians are viewed as self-interested whether they tell the truth or not. The blurriness of news and opinion and the media's role in providing a platform for unmoderated and anonymous comments diminishes the very important role that journalism plays in a society. Citizens need to realize that it is worth paying for accurate, reliable journalism. The very business model of many traditional news organizations is under threat. Catering to 'getting eyeballs' in a highly competitive news marketplace has fed sensationalism and news as infotainment.

The news media need to take on a new role as the curators and aggregators of the truth. With fake news and lies in politics, the trusted traditional media have a new business opportunity: Simply to tell citizens that if they tune in to the news or subscribe to the newspaper, they will get the truth. The news will be aggregated and curated and opinion should be clearly delineated from news. Citizens need to realize that it is worth paying for accurate, reliable journalism. This will not only require a remake of the business model of news; it will also require elevating the profession by investing in journalism schools. It will not be enough to repair the media business model. The next generation of journalists must be ready to take on their very important roles, not only for their news organizations but for democracy.

Creating opportunities for more citizen education

The data suggests the key emerging division when it comes to anger politics is not necessarily gender, race, or income. Men, women, young, old, rich and poor are angry and feel that society is on the decline. The research suggests that education could very well be the emerging acute dividing line in society akin to many of the dystopian science fiction novels with a technology and knowledge-based caste system – a world divided between the haves and the have-nots.

Those with a lower educational attainment are more likely to want to punish the establishment or see change. Likewise, in a world economy defined by globalization and trade, citizens with a lower educational attainment, regardless of income, likely feel more at risk in terms of their ability to adapt to a changing global marketplace and a perceived 'savage globalization', as coined by right-wing French politician Marine Le Pen.

The increase in cost of post-secondary education in many developed nations and weakened access exacerbates the education dividing line. Tuition rates in many, although not all, countries are rising, and students are increasingly expected to bear a greater burden of the true cost of education. There has been significant research done on the relationship between educational attainment and voter turnout. The higher the educational attainment, the greater the likelihood to vote.

Investing in greater citizen access to post-secondary education has a potential two-pronged long-term positive impact. First, it could increase voter turnout. Second, it could help break down the emerging two solitudes on democratic dialogue. Third, it may help advance a sense of greater personal economic control for citizens. For those with a lower educational attainment, the globalization of trade and automation of the workplace is transformation which takes away personal control over one's economic future. Change, less control, and perceived threats from abroad tap into a personal angst where voters look to politicians promising to take back control of borders, immigration, and trade relationships.

FACTS
MYTHS
NEWS

CONCLUDING THOUGHTS

Threats such as algorithm-influenced and data-driven bots are key enablers of fake news and distorted democratic dialogue. Cheap, accessible and immediate in their impact, they are a destabilizing influence and create a false reality for citizens and for the media trying to understand the mood of society. Coupled with the reality of how small swings of voters influence outcomes and governing style, this angry tail wags to punish.

This new age of voter rage, enabled by technology and social media, is rewiring democracy. It is reshaping party systems across a number of democracies as parties either choose to adapt or fail. At the same time, it is renewing interest and engagement in democracy as politics becomes a mix of national policy dialogue and reality TV entertainment where through social media, everyone can be a participant. However, it is the spread and use of computational propaganda, bots and algorithms that are blurring the line between truth and falsehood, and between reliable and fake news. How can elections reliably capture the will of the people, if enough views are shaped by falsehoods to influence democratic outcomes and the politicians chosen to lead nations?

These proposed treatments are neither short-term nor easy. They are intended to address some of the fundamental problems besetting democracy. Racism, xenophobia, the willingness to accept or ignore political lies, distrust of the political order, and fear of trade are symptoms of a more fundamental problem: The view of some citizens that the system is failing them. In that respect, the age of voter rage and the tyranny of small numbers is about dealing with marginalized citizens – those who believe their livelihood and the livelihood of their children may be at risk. Populist-style politicians engaging in demagogic rhetoric tap into the marginalized citizenry and know that very small swings can significantly shape outcomes. The reality is that democratic outcomes and the stability of governments are much more fragile than a vote once every four years or so would suggest.

Society is increasingly in a post-partisan, post-truth world, where the lines between real news and fake news, between entertainment and politics, between celebrity and statesman are blurred. Populist-style politics in many instances is more about punishing the establishment than advancing coherent policy options, and it is on the rise. Independently minded voters, less loyal to parties, are increasing in numbers. As citizens become less partisan and less engaged in formal political parties, those parties on the left and the right have fewer but more extreme party members. The next generation of dividing lines may not be ideological but between the centre and the fringes on both left and right, as witnessed in the 2017 French election.

The Internet is an enabler of fringe and non-mainstream opinion and beliefs. Social media is the turbo-charged jet engine, rocketing opinions, mistruths, facts and counter facts in snappy 140-character political consumables. Now if a politician makes a mistake or speaks out of turn, it is propelled so quickly that it is difficult to retrieve or correct. So what do politicians do? They let it ride. To paraphrase Al Gore, it is an 'inconvenient truth'[81]. The post-truth era is further strained by a media industry looking to remake its business model. In a competitive fast-paced environment, in newsrooms low on resources, stories searching for eyeballs are pushed out the door.

The disruption in TV consumption habits with the rise of YouTube and Netflix has begun to restructure broadcast television to focus more on live events. Sports and politics remain, to one extent, the last continuous stream of live experiences. 'Give them bread and circuses'[82] was the old adage for a quick rise to power attributed to the Roman poet Juvenal. The 2016 US election was much like that. The campaign was a steady stream of live news, entertainment and happenings, 24 hours a day, seven days a week. One can argue that the Trump presidency in the US is a seven-days-a-week, 24-hours-a-day live TV event which has transfixed, both positively and negatively, voters in America. The intersection of entertainment, democracy, untruthfulness and economic anxiety makes

81 Gore, A. (n.d.). An Inconvenient Truth (Movie). Retrieved July 6, 2017, from https://www.algore.com/library/an-inconvenient-truth-dvd.

82 Latin 'Panem et Circensus': attributed to Juvenal. Retrieved July 6, 2017 from http://www.capitolium.org/eng/imperatori/circenses.htm.

the anger of nations a powerful new force remaking democracy.

This newest wave of populist-style politics is different from the past. It is high velocity, tinged by anger, driven by minority opinion and propelled by computational propaganda in the semblance of social media and human interaction. Fast and loose with the facts at times, it has a backdrop of economic woe and is open to manipulation by social media enabled algorithms. It makes and keeps voters angry. Politicians like US President Donald Trump are partly ideological but more contrarian in nature – disrupting and unbalancing the political and media establishments is the name of the game. Unseating enemies helps unsettle their natural advantages and helps the disruptor. Anti-establishment politics in a sense is a communications perpetual motion machine. When an anti-establishment politician delivers on a promise, it is a political win. When blocked or frustrated, the establishment is blamed as obstructive, thus validating the angry assertion that the system is broken.

Donald Trump may be frustrated by Congress in making good on his election promises. In the case where his agenda is frustrated, he will in fact have more fodder to remind his political tribe how 'broken' Washington is and that the problem is much deeper than he anticipated. In that sense, one should not dismiss any difficulty he has in implementing his agenda as a set-back – a set-back reinforces his anti-establishment message.

Some may take solace when a populist anger movement of the extreme right or left does not win, but the creeping rage of voters should not be underestimated. It signals that the fundamental diagnosis of disconnectedness, disaffectedness and economic pessimism has not been addressed. The age of voter rage brings into question how democracy works, whether it works and who it works for. For those reasons, this reflection is a beginning of an understanding, a first but not a last word.

POLITICAL TIMELINES

June 16th, 2015	Trump declares candidacy for Republican Party
August 2nd, 2015	Canadian Election called – Liberals and Trudeau trailing incumbent Conservative Government
October 19th, 2015	Liberal Leader Trudeau win majority in Canadian House of Commons
April 6th, 2016	French politician Macron creates his own new political party En Marche!
May 3rd, 2016	Trump becomes presumptive Republican nominee
June 23rd, 2016	UK Narrowly votes in favour Brexit, within 90 minutes of result, Brexit campaigners begin Back-pedalling on signature promise to reclaim £350M repatriation for the National Health Service
November 8th, 2016	Trump wins US Electoral College but loses popular vote
November 16th, 2016	Macron declares candidacy to be President of France
March 15th, 2017	Incumbent government wins Dutch election but right-wing Party for Freedom (PVV) picks up more seats in legislature
April 18th, 2017	UK Election called – May-led Conservatives lead in the polls
April 23rd, 2017	First round of French Presidential Election takes place – with only five percent gap

	between the top four candidates – Macron and LePen move to second round.
May 7th, 2017	Second round of French Presidential Election takes place – Macron defeats LePen
May 22nd, 2017	UK Conservative PM May withdraws platform promise on controversy dubbed the 'dementia tax'
May 22nd, 2017	Tragic terror attack in Manchester during UK Election
June 8th, 2017	May-led Conservative Party loses majority in UK House of Commons but governs with a new minority
September 24th, 2017	Chancellor Angela Merkel wins election but the right wing Alternative for Germany (AfD) almost triples popular support.

ACKNOWLEDGEMENTS

There are times when one must believe in serendipity.

It was Monday November 7th 2016, the day before the epic US presidential election showdown between Trump and Clinton. That grey day I broke bread with my friend and former university debating opponent Todd Swift at the Galvin Bistro Deluxe on Baker Street in London. With a friendship forged on the Canadian university debating circuit, we were checking in after a long hiatus, catching up and talking politics. As we hashed out the Brexit vote and talked about the US election, it was Todd who broached the topic of me writing a book on this phenomenon that had swept the United Kingdom and was transfixing the American voting public.

The next day Trump was transformed from media phenomenon to president of the United States.

After a fury of emails, Todd and I reconvened within 48 hours at the Starbucks near the Maida Vale tube station and, fortified with espresso, we reached a deal. With that, I thank my friend and publisher Todd Swift for making this book a reality. To his team at Eyewear Publishing – Alexandra Payne and Edwin Smet have been superb to deal with – thank you all.

On the home front back in Canada, I would like to thank my wife Paule Labbé, who not only indulged me in this writing endeavor but who was my reliable and insightful sounding board. It doesn't get much better than that. She is my life and intellectual partner. And how could I not thank the Flying Nanos Brothers (my four boys), James, Greg, Paul and Marc, who were on the receiving end of many questions about what they thought about Donald Trump and politics in the United States?

It would be remiss for me to not also thank my brother and business partner John, who silently and patiently allowed me to spend time on this project.

One of the key tenets in this book is that a big part of the voter rage is driven by declinism – that people are pessimistic about their own economic upward mobility and believe that their children might not have the same standard of living as them. Part of the antidote for declinism is a society and political system where individuals have opportunities to grow and thrive. And with that my last thank you is to Canada. Who would have thought that some kid, the son of Greek immigrants, brought up by a single mom, born in Canada, not speaking English until he went to kindergarten, would have the honor of doing research and giving voice to citizens. Go figure.

INDEX

OUR OTHER TITLES IN THE SQUINT SERIES

Squint Books focus on the 21st Century Digital Age, from Pop Culture to Politics, Art to Science, with an emphasis on Key Figures

BARACK OBAMA – INVISIBLE MAN

DONALD TRUMP – THE RHETORIC

THE EVOLUTION OF HILLARY RODHAM CLINTON

JEREMY CORBYN – ACCIDENTAL HERO

JUSTIN TRUDEAU – CANADA'S SELFIE PM

TACTICAL READING: A SNAPPY GUIDE TO THE SNAP GENERAL ELECTION 2017

ROGER FEDERER – PORTRAIT OF AN ARTIST

THE FRAGILE DEMOCRACY

HOW TO DO PRIVACY IN THE 21ST CENTURY

ADELE – THE OTHER SIDE

LANA DEL REY – HER LIFE IN 94 SONGS

WWW.EYEWEARPUBLISHING.COM